# The Right to be Forgotten

Exploring the evolution of the right to be forgotten, its challenges, and its impact on privacy, reputation, and online expression, this book lays out the current state of the law on the right to be forgotten in Canada and in the international context while addressing the broader theoretical tensions at its core.

The essays contemplate questions such as: How does the right to be forgotten fit into existing legal frameworks? How can Canadian courts and policy-makers reconcile rights to privacy and rights to access publicly available information? Should search engines be regulated purely as commercial actors? What is the right's impact on free speech and freedom of the press? Together, these essays address the questions that legal actors and policy-makers must consider as they move forward in shaping this new right through legislation, regulations, and jurisprudence. They address both the difficulties in introducing the right and the long-term effects it could have on the protection of online (and offline) reputation and speech. As the question of implementing the right to be forgotten in Canada has been put forward by the Privacy Commissioner and considered by courts, Canada is in need of academic literature on the matter; a need that, with this book, we intend to fulfill.

The questions put forward in this book will thus advance the legal debate in Canada and provide a rich case study for the international legal community.

**Ignacio N. Cofone** is an Assistant Professor at McGill University Faculty of Law, where he teaches Privacy Law, and an Affiliated Fellow at the Yale Law School Information Society Project. His research explores how the law should adapt to technological and social change with a focus on privacy and algorithmic decision-making.

# The Right to be Forgotten
## A Canadian and Comparative Perspective

**Edited by**
**Ignacio N. Cofone**

Routledge
Taylor & Francis Group

LONDON AND NEW YORK

First published 2020
by Routledge
2 Park Square, Milton Park, Abingdon, Oxon OX14 4RN

and by Routledge
605 Third Avenue, New York, NY 10017

First issued in paperback 2021

*Routledge is an imprint of the Taylor & Francis Group, an informa business*

Publisher's Note
The publisher has gone to great lengths to ensure the quality of this reprint but points out that some imperfections in the original copies may be apparent.

*British Library Cataloguing-in-Publication Data*
A catalogue record for this book is available from the British Library

*Library of Congress Cataloging-in-Publication Data*
Names: Privacy Revolution (Conference) (2018: McGill University Centre for Intellectual Property Policy) |
Cofone, Ignacio N., 1987– editor.
Title: The right to be forgotten: A Canadian and comparative perspective / edited by Ignacio N Cofone.
Description: Abingdon, Oxon; New York, NY: Routledge, 2020. | Includes bibliographical references and index.
Identifiers: LCCN 2019055052 (print) | LCCN 2019055053 (ebook) | ISBN 9780367859749 (hardback) | ISBN 9781003017011 (ebook)
Subjects: LCSH: Right to be forgotten—Canada—Congresses. | Right to be forgotten—Congresses.
Classification: LCC KE1242.C6 .P75 2020 (print) | LCC KE1242.C6 (ebook) | DDC 323.44/80971—dc23
LC record available at https://lccn.loc.gov/2019055052
LC ebook record available at https://lccn.loc.gov/2019055053

ISBN 13: 978-1-03-223858-6 (pbk)
ISBN 13: 978-0-367-85974-9 (hbk)

Typeset in Times New Roman
by codeMantra

# Contents

# Acknowledgments

This book and the essays it contains were born out of academic exchanges between participants at the *Privacy Revolution* conference organized in 2019. I owe special thanks to the Centre for Intellectual Property Policy at McGill University, which provided an essential framework to put together such an event and this book, and especially to its director, Pierre-Emmanuel Moyse. I also gratefully acknowledge the generous support of the Caroline Bérubé and Jean Gabriel Castel funds at McGill University. More broadly, I am grateful for the institutional support of the Faculty of Law and Dean Robert Leckey. A special mention is owed to ten anonymous peer reviewers, who I cannot credit by name but who provided useful feedback to the authors and myself within each chapter and for the book as a whole. Finally, and most importantly, three stellar law students and research assistants from McGill University Faculty of Law, Francis Langlois, Cédrick Mulcair, and Ana Qarri, provided invaluable help at every stage of the process.

# Contributors

**Ignacio N. Cofone** is an Assistant Professor at McGill University, Faculty of Law, and an Affiliated Fellow at the Yale Law School Information Society Project.

**Pierre-Luc Déziel** is an Assistant Professor at Laval University, Faculty of Law.

**Teresa Scassa** is a Professor and Canada Research Chair in Information Law and Policy at the University of Ottawa, Faculty of Law.

**Andrea Slane** is a Professor of Law at the University of Ontario Institute of Technology, Faculty of Social Science and Humanities.

**Jennifer Stoddart** is the Former Privacy Commissioner of Canada and a Strategic Advisor at the Fasken Privacy and Cybersecurity Group.

**Catalina Turriago Betancourt** is an attorney and a graduate student at McGill University, Faculty of Law.

# 1 Online harms and the right to be forgotten

*Ignacio N. Cofone*

## 1 Introduction

The idea of a right to delete one's personal information was popularized by Mayer-Schönberger's book *Delete* and its story about Stacy Snyder.[1] Snyder was studying to become a high-school teacher when one of her professors found a picture she had posted on a social network website in which she was drinking from a plastic cup while wearing a pirate hat, captioned "drunken pirate." After the professor contacted the university authorities, she was said to be expelled.[2] She sued to reverse that decision but failed.[3] Through Snyder's story – one that is certainly not unique – Mayer-Schönberger proposed the wide implementation of a new privacy right: the right to delete information about ourselves.[4]

Mayer-Schönberger argued that one of the main problems of electronic data processing and storage is that it lacks the human characteristic of forgetting,[5] which he highlighted as a human characteristic with an important social function. Before the existence of large-scale information technologies that facilitate quick and easy access to publicly available information, true information about individuals held by others faded with time. Consequently, the weight that negative or embarrassing information about people had on their reputation generally lessened with time, allowing them to restore their

1 Viktor Mayer-Schönberger, *Delete: The Virtue of Forgetting in the Digital Age* (Woodstock: Princeton University Press, 2009) at 1–15.
2 This frequent reconstruction is actually inaccurate. See Jack Herlocker, "Sidney Snyder and the Untruth that Won't Die" *Medium* (21 September 2015). See also *Stacey Snyder v Millersville University et al.*, U.S. Dist. LEXIS 97943 (ED Pa 2008).
3 Ibid.
4 Mayer-Schönberger, *supra* note 1 at 1–15.
5 Ibid at 92–127.

reputation. He thus proposed "the right to forget," meaning that personal information should have expiry dates after which it would be deleted automatically.[6]

Another story that motivated debate and turned into a landmark decision that created law is that of Mario Costeja. Costeja requested Google and a Spanish newspaper to eliminate an article which reported a government auction on his house. The opinion of the European Court of Justice (ECJ) advocate general stated that the current European legal framework does not provide a right to eliminate truthful but embarrassing information.[7] But the ECJ disagreed,[8] ordering Google Spain to delist the content from search results and stating that search engines must delist content that is "inadequate, irrelevant or no longer relevant, or excessive."[9]

Since the 2014 *Google Spain* decision, the right to be forgotten (RTBF) has been the locus of extensive academic debate across the globe and is one of the most contested legal innovations in the realm of privacy. Since its formal recognition, the right has raised important questions about how, in the face of networked technology, legal systems balance privacy, reputation, and free speech.

## 2  What is the right to be forgotten?

The idea of a right to forget one's information originally comes from the French *droit à l'oubli* and the Italian *diritto al' oblio* for criminal records – sometimes called right to oblivion, and literally translatable as right to forget.[10] These types of rights focused on erasing court or government records after a certain amount of time. They were affirmed by courts based on constitutional dispositions about the social reinsertion aims

6  Ibid at 169–195.
7  This opinion was based on the interpretation of article 2(b) of the Data Protection Directive given by the ECJ in *Lindqvist*. See *Bodil Lindqvist v. Åklagarkammaren i Jönköping*, C-101/01, [2003] ECR I-12971. Attorney Generals are appointed members to the ECJ that do not render judicial decisions and are not privy to the deliberations of judges. Their principal function is to draft legal opinions in relation to specific cases. See Philippe Léger, "Law in the European Union: The Role of the Advocate General" (2004) 10:1 J of Legislative Studies 1.
8  See *Google Spain SL and Google Inc v Agencia Española de Protección de Datos (AEPD) and Mario Costeja González*, CJEU C-131/12, [2014] ECR I-317, EUR-Lex CELEX No 62012CJ0131.
9  Ibid at para 93.
10  See W. Gregory Voss & Celine Castets-Renard, "Proposal for an International Taxonomy on the Various Forms of the 'Right to Be Forgotten': A Study on the Convergence of Norms" (2016) 14 Colorado Technology L J 281 at 299–302.

of prison punishments, stating that it is in the interest of both social re-insertion and the privacy of people who were convicted for the records to be erased after some time.[11] The RTBF takes a similar logic for a much wider set of information.[12]

The European Union (EU) was sympathetic to this idea.[13] Instead of the right to forget, which would focus on the expiration of information after some time, the European Commission led by then EU Commissioner Viviane Reding proposed in the General Data Protection Regulation (GDPR) to include the RTBF,[14] which normatively focuses on the control over one's personal information.[15]

As a result, the right is now in article 17 of the GDPR. As stipulated in article 17, the right establishes that people can demand information about themselves to be deleted by entities that collect or process their personal data.[16] This extends the right of data subjects beyond those granted in *Google Spain*.[17] It allows them, subject to balancing with other rights such as free speech, to request any data controller, at any time, to eliminate from their databases any piece of information regarding that data subject, regardless of the source of the information, and regardless of whether that information produces harm.[18]

---

11 See Martine Herzog-Evans, "Judicial Rehabilitation in France: Helping with the Desisting Process and Acknowledging Achieved Desistance" (2011) European J of Probation 3.1 at 4–19; Steven Bennett, "The 'Right to Be Forgotten': Reconciling EU and US Perspectives" (2012) 30 Berkeley J Intl L 161; Alessandro Mantelero, "The EU Proposal for a General Data Protection Regulation and the Roots of the 'Right to be Forgotten'" (2013) 29 Computer L Security Rev 229.

12 See Jennifer Stoddart, "Lost in Translation: Transposing the Right to be Forgotten from Different Legal Systems" (Chapter 2) for more details.

13 See Jeffrey Rosen, "The Right to be Forgotten" (2012) 64 Stan L Rev 88 at 89.

14 In EU law, regulations are pieces of legislation that are directly applicable internally, as opposed to directives, which must be implemented by each member state. While directives are used to harmonize EU law, regulations are used to unify it.

15 See Rolf Weber, "The Right to Be Forgotten More Than a Pandora's Box?" (2011) 2 J of Intellectual Property, Information Technology and Electronic Commerce L 120.

16 See Viviane Reding, "The Upcoming Data Protection Reform for the European Union" (2011) 1 Intl Data Privacy L 3.

17 This is the term used by European data protection law for people whose data are being collected or processed. See e.g. EC, *Regulation (EU) 2016/679* of 27 April 2016 on the protection of natural persons with regard to the processing of personal data and on the free movement of such data, and repealing Directive 95/46/EC (General Data Protection Regulation), [2016] OJ, L 119 at 33 ("'personal data' means any information relating to an identified or identifiable natural person ('data subject')") [GDPR].

18 See Ignacio N. Cofone, "Google v. Spain: A Right to be Forgotten?" (2015) 15 Chicago-Kent JICL 1.

The RTBF, therefore, has been deemed to mean any of two things. The two meanings of the RTBF are the right to delete information about oneself, often called erasure, and the right to remove information about one in search engine results, often called delisting.[19] The first type – the right to erasure – is recognized in article 17 of the GDPR.[20] The second type was recognized in *Google Spain* and is more frequently applied in other jurisdictions that recognize some version of the RTBF than is the first.[21] As the subsequent chapters show, these two versions have different implications for rights such as free speech and access to information.

Each of these two versions of the right can also exist at three different levels. First, and least controversially, the RTBF can mean that one has the right to delete or delist information that one posts online.[22] Many, but not all, websites and social network sites allow for this. Second, it can mean that one has the right to delete or delink information about oneself that one originally posted online, including information that others have re-posted later on, reproducing one's initial post.[23] This seems to be the intention of commissioner Reding when proposing the right, based on some early statements.[24] Third, it can mean that one has the right to delete or delink information that is available online about oneself, regardless of its origin.[25] This is the scope of the RTBF in article 17 of the GDPR.[26]

19 Voss & Castets-Renard, *supra* note 10 at 302–337; Andrea Slane, "Search Engines and the Right to Be Forgotten: Squaring the Remedy with Canadian Values on Personal Information Flow" (2018) 55 Osgoode Hall L Rev 349 at 358.
20 See generally F. Brimblecombe & G. Phillipson, "Regaining Digital Privacy? The New 'Right to be Forgotten' and Online Expression" (2018) 4 Can J of Comparative and Contemporary L 1.
21 See Pierre Luc-Déziel, "Let's Not Dwell on The Past: The Right to Be Forgotten as More Than a Romantic Revolution" (Chapter 5) for more details.
22 See Peter Fleischer, "Foggy Thinking about the Right to Oblivion" *Peter Fleischer: Privacy...?* (9 March 2011), online: http://peterfleischer.blogspot.com/2011/03/foggy-thinking-about-right-to-oblivion.html; Rosen, *supra* note 13; Michael Rustad & Sanna Kulevkam, "Reconceptualizing the Right to be Forgotten to Enable Transatlantic Data Flow" (2015) 28 Harv JL & Tech 349 at 387–398.
23 Ibid.
24 See Viviane Reding, "The Future of Data Protection and Transatlantic Cooperation" (Speech delivered at 2nd Annual European Data Protection and Privacy Conference, 6 December 2011); John Hendel, "Why Journalists Shouldn't Fear Europe's "Right to be Forgotten", *The Atlantic* (25 January 2012).
25 *Supra* note 22.
26 See GDPR, art 17.1(b) ("the data subject withdraws consent on which the processing is based").

## 3 Online harms

What is the problem that the RTBF is trying to solve? To understand its motivation, it is important to understand what it is trying to fix. The RTBF is important because it exists as a remedy for online harms.

The right that is often highlighted as central to the RTBF is privacy. However, the right to privacy is inextricably tied to values such as personal autonomy, dignity, and individuality.[27] It comes as no surprise then that harms to privacy are inextricably tied to a host of other harms. Online interactions include such distinct set of harms. Namely, among others: reputational harm (e.g. when employers find inaccurate information about a job candidate), financial harm (e.g. with identity theft), discriminatory harm (e.g. when a member of a non-visible minority is "outed"), bodily harm (e.g. when someone is doxed and then harassed), harm to autonomy (e.g. when someone's personal information is used to manipulate them), and privacy harm.

The stories of Stacy Snyder and Mario Costeja can be seen as examples of reputational harm. But online harms to reputation can be much more serious when issued within efforts of online harassment. Targeted individuals of these online disclosures are often subject to significant emotional damage, and "feel anxiety and shame every time they see the postings or learn that others have seen them."[28] When women are victims, these often involve publicly accusing them of engaging in sex work or carrying sexually transmitted infections.[29] Reputational harm is particularly pernicious when it leads not only to emotional harm but also to an interference with the victim's daily life; when, to ensure their reputation is not damaged further, the onus turns onto them to not do things they would normally do. For example, victims are often forced to stay offline and close their accounts in order not to provoke their harassers.[30] In some cases, such as in the story of Monica Lewinsky, they cannot go in public without facing some replication of the original harassment.[31] Like Ari Waldman puts it, "online harassment is particularly pernicious because it is cheap, fast and permanent."[32]

---

27 Daniel J. Solove, "Conceptualizing Privacy" (2002) 90 Cal L Rev 1087 at 1117.
28 Danielle Keats Citron, "Mainstreaming Privacy Torts" (2010) 98 Cal L Rev 1805 at 1814.
29 Danielle Keats Citron, *Hate Crimes in Cyberspace* (Cambridge, MA: Harvard University Press, 2014) at 24–46.
30 Ibid at 44.
31 Monica Lewinsky, "The Price of Shame", *TED Talk* (20 March 2015).
32 Ari Waldman, "Cybermobs Multiply Online Threats and Their Danger", *New York Times* (3 August 2016).

The second type of harm is financial. Examples of online financial harm are identity theft enabled by stolen personal information,[33] facilitation of fraud,[34] raised premiums,[35] and price discrimination.[36] While these harms also exist offline, networked technology facilitates and magnifies them.[37] A notorious example of this is the Equifax breach, which in 2018 lost financial information of an estimated 143 million taxpayers – an amount of information that, in the past, no private company would have.[38] Information brokers, similarly, sell data that are sometimes incomplete or inaccurate, which when sold to potential employers cost people jobs.[39] Most online financial harms have their consequences in the long-run, which makes it difficult to anticipate how much financial damage took place at the moment of the interaction: a stolen social security number may lead to identity theft years later, and price discrimination, raise of insurance premiums, and loss of job opportunities occur as a result of a long and obscure process where it is difficult for the victim to identify the source of harm.

The third is discrimination: when members of historically disadvantaged groups are unjustly treated differently due to their group membership in an online environment. Discrimination works similarly online and offline, with the difference being that the same technologies that amplify reputational harm can amplify discriminatory harm, for example, when a platform allows its users to make decisions on the basis of race.[40] Regulations are often designed to block access to people's personal information to prevent them from being discriminated against, for example, when employment law forbids employers from asking female job candidates whether they intend to take maternity leave during employment[41] or when genetic nondiscrimination statutes

33  Citron, *supra* note 28 at 1815.
34  Marshall Allen, "Health Insurers Are Vacuuming Up Details about You — And It Could Raise Your Rates", *ProPublica* (17 July 2018).
35  Justin Brookman & GS Hans, "Why Collection Matters: Surveillance as a De Facto Privacy Harm", *Centre for Democracy and Technology* (8 September 2013) at 2.
36  Vincent Conitzer, Curtis R. Taylor & Liad Wagman, "Hide and Seek: Costly Consumer Privacy in a Market with Repeat Purchases" (2012) 31:2 Marketing Science 277.
37  Citron, *supra* note 28 at 1816.
38  Zack Whittaker, "Equifax Breach Was 'Entirely Preventable' Had It used Basic Security Measures, Says House Report", *TechCrunch* (10 December 2018).
39  Citron, *supra* note 28 at 1816.
40  *Fair Housing Council of San Fernando Valley v. Roommates.com LLC*, 521 F (3d) 1157 (9th Cir 2008).
41  Ignacio N. Cofone, "Antidiscriminatory Privacy" (2019) 72 SMU L Rev 139.

prevent employers from acquiring genetic information about their employees.[42] When people's personal information is processed by decision-making algorithms, this also leads to distinct forms of algorithmic discrimination that have a larger scale than human discrimination and are often hidden behind promises of neutrality.[43]

The fourth harm is to physical integrity. Online abuse often leads to cyberharassment or cyberstalking that includes physical harm, such as battery, or the threat of physical harm, often including threats of rape or death.[44] When queer people are involved, it sometimes involves non-consensual pornography or their impersonation to send people who are looking for sex to their home or work.[45] Online abuse often involves doxxing, which leads to abuse by others.[46] Particularly, online harms to physical integrity are disproportionately suffered by women.[47]

The fifth type of harm is online manipulation, which can be defined as the use of technology to "covertly influence another person's decision-making, by targeting and exploiting their decision-making vulnerabilities."[48] People's personal data, in particular, can be used to influence their decisions. In recent years, for example, there have been reported cases of political campaigns meaningfully influencing voters' choices,[49] including the Cambridge Analytica scandal. More broadly, what Shoshana Zuboff calls "behavior modification," which relates to

42 Jessica L. Roberts, "Protecting Privacy to Prevent Discrimination" (2014) 56 Wm & Mary L Rev 2097 at 2146; Ignacio N. Cofone, "Nothing to Hide, but Something to Lose" (2019) 70:1 UTLJ 64.

43 Solon Barocas & Andrew D. Selbst, "Big Data's Disparate Impact" (2016) 104 Cal L Rev 671; Ignacio N. Cofone, "Algorithmic Discrimination is an Information Problem" (2019) 70:6 Hastings LJ 1389.

44 Citron, *supra* note 29 at 5–8; Mary Anne Franks, "*Sexual Harassment 2.0*" (2012) 71 Md L Rev 655 at 657–658.

45 See generally Ari Waldman, "Queer Dating Apps Are Unsafe by Design: Privacy Is Particularly Important for L.G.B.T.Q. People", *New York Times* (20 June 2019); *Matthew Herrick v Grindr Inc*, 765 Fed Appx 586 (2nd Cir 2019).

46 Nellie Veronika Binder, "From the Message Board to the Front Door: Addressing the Offline Consequences of Race- and Gender-Based Doxxing and Swatting" (2018) 51 Suffolk UL Rev 55 at 58.

47 Danielle Keats Citron, "Sexual Privacy" (2019) 128 Yale LJ 1870.

48 Daniel Susser, Beate Roessler & Helen Nissenbaum, "Technology, Autonomy, and Manipulation" (2019) 8:2 Internet Policy Rev 1.

49 Siva Vaidhyanathan, *Antisocial Media: How Facebook Disconnects Us and Undermines Democracy* (Oxford: Oxford University Press, 2018); Frederik Zuiderveen Borgesius et al., "Online Political Microtargeting: Promises and Threats for Democracy" (2018) 14:1 Utrecht L Rev 82.

buying things we do not need or want,[50] is a pervasive business model central to the information economy.[51] For some, this online environment involves harms to autonomy of varying magnitude.[52]

The last, and perhaps most important, type of online harm that the RTBF is concerned with is privacy harm. That is, invasion of privacy and its intertwined moral and psychological harms. Across different normative conceptions,[53] privacy usually refers either to the control of one's personal information, to limiting access to such information, or to its contextual integrity.[54] These views aim to identify when privacy is diminished, rather than when privacy rights are breached, so they relate more closely than do normative conceptions to identifying harms to privacy. "Describing the outer boundaries and core properties of privacy harm helps to reveal values, identify and address new problems, and guard against dilution."[55]

In the past, invasion of privacy was addressed through "bread and butter" lawsuits. People sued when someone opened their letters, broke into their house and went through their diary, or disclosed details about them breaking professional secrecy. The internet introduced a host of new, privacy-related, online harms. But next to them, online interactions continue to produce a distinct type of harm that society already recognized with opening of letters and professional secrecy, just in a new technological context: protecting us from others learning intimate facts about us that we do not want them to know. This is what privacy harm is.[56] "Just as a burn is an injury caused by heat, so is privacy harm a unique injury with specific boundaries and characteristics."[57]

Identifying privacy harm is important precisely because of its intrinsic relation with other online harms. When a website makes a ghost profile with someone's name on it but the individual lacks evidence of reputational damage, courts are unsure of whether to grant

50 Tal Zarsky, "Privacy and Manipulation in the Digital Age" (2019) 20:1 Theor Inq L 157; Ryan Calo, "Digital Market Manipulation" (2014) 82:4 Geo Wash L Rev 995.
51 Shoshana Zuboff, *The Age of Surveillance Capitalism: The Fight for a Human Future at the New Frontier of Power* (New York: Public Affairs Books, 2019).
52 Susser et al., *supra* note 48.
53 Solove, *supra* note 27 at 1099–1121.
54 Helen Nissenbaum, *Privacy in Context: Technology, Policy, and the Integrity of Social Life* (Stanford: Stanford University Press, 2010) at 67–126.
55 Ryan Calo, "The Boundaries of Privacy Harm" (2011) 86:3 Ind LJ 2 at 1142.
56 Ignacio N. Cofone & Adriana Robertson, "Privacy Harms" (2018) 69 Hastings LJ 1039; Ignacio N. Cofone & Adriana Robertson, "Consumer Privacy in a Behavioral World" (2018) 69 Hastings LJ 1471.
57 Calo, *supra* note 55 at 1142.

her remedy.[58] The same is true when a credit bureau is hacked but victims lack evidence that this caused them financial damage.[59] Likewise, that is true when women and queer people share compromising pictures that are then disseminated.[60] The recognition of privacy harm in those situations gives victims some sort of redress.

The RTBF, while closely tied to the right to privacy, is a distinct right that seeks to address a wide universe of online harms. Key to people's privacy interests in an online environment, it also shelters their reputation, finances, physical integrity, nondiscrimination, and autonomy.

## 4 The importance of the Canadian perspective

### 4.1 It's far from over: legislative and policy debates

By bringing together original work on the RTBF, the authors in this book critically assess whether and how legislators and courts can and should conceptualize the RTBF in Canada. Through the perspectives of academics and practitioners, the book asks how the RTBF fits into the Canadian legal framework as a means to explore the various theoretical tensions present in different permutations of the right's implementation.

This is a pivotal moment for Canada's way forward in balancing online speech, privacy, and reputation, as it is unclear where the balance will be struck as courts, Parliament, and the Office of the Privacy Commissioner consider its introduction into the Canadian legal framework. The question of whether the *Personal Information Protection and Electronic Documents Act* (PIPEDA) applies to search engines will be under legislative review with the proposed modernization of PIPEDA.[61] As Canada's adequacy standing under the GDPR will soon be reviewed, the Canadian government is working with the

---

58 *Spokeo Inc v Robins*, 136 S. Ct. 1540 (2016).
59 Bloomberg Editorial Board, "The Unfinished Business of the Equifax Hack", *Bloomberg* (29 January 2019).
60 Scott Skinner-Thompson, "Privacy's Double Standards" (2018) 93:4 Wash L Rev 2051.
61 Innovation, Science and Economic Development Canada, "Strengthening Privacy in the Digital Age: Proposals to modernize the *Personal Information Protection and Electronic Documents Act*", Government of Canada (21 May 2019); Office of the Privacy Commissioner of Canada, Announcement, "Privacy Commissioner Seeks Federal Court Determination on Key Issue for Canadians' Online Reputation" (10 October 2018).

European Commission to evaluate the requirements of the GDPR's essential equivalence standard,[62] which may involve incorporating some version of the RTBF.

Moreover, a Reference currently before the Federal Court leaves open the possibility that PIPEDA will be found to apply to the search function of search engines, which would introduce a right to delist.[63] While PIPEDA does recognize some very limited rights to deletion (correction and accuracy), it does not have a right comparable to erasure.[64] The Standing Committee on Access to Information, Privacy and Ethics, which released its review of PIPEDA in 2018, recommended that PIPEDA should include a more comprehensive data erasure regime as well as a right to delist. As the report points out, while PIPEDA allows individuals to delete information they post themselves (the first level as described above), it does not allow them to demand deletion of information posted by third parties. This leaves little redress for online harms caused by this situation, like in cases of cyberbullying or non-consensual pornography.

### 4.2  What the Canadian framework can say about the right abroad

The book uses Canada as a case study to draw broader normative considerations that aim to be applicable in different parts of the world. To do so, it rests on speech and privacy norms, transsystemic approaches to law, and extraterritoriality.

The two jurisdictions that have been at the center of the academic debate on the RTBF so far – the United States (US) and the EU – have drastically different approaches to privacy and its relationship to free speech. The EU has stronger privacy norms than most other jurisdictions, while the US has stronger free speech norms than most

62 See Innovation, Science, and Economic Development Canada, "Letter from the Minister to the Standing Committee on Access to Information, Privacy and Ethics" (7 November 2019) at 8.
63 See Teresa Scassa, "A Little Knowledge Is a Dangerous Thing?: Information Asymmetries and the Right to Be Forgotten" (Chapter 3) for more details.
64 House of Commons, *Towards Privacy by Design: Report of the Standing Committee on Access, Information, Privacy, and Ethics* (February 2018) (Chair: Bob Zimmer) at 37. See Andrea Slane, "Reconciling Privacy and Expression Rights by Regulating Profile Compilation Services" (Chapter 4) for more details.

countries.[65] Canada's speech and privacy norms fall between those of the EU and the US.[66] In the words of Gratton and Polonetsky,

> Canada, on the issue of freedom of expression and privacy, has a balanced legal framework. While the Canadian Charter of Rights provides [strong] constitutional protection to fundamental freedoms such as freedom of expression, Canada has also adopted data protection laws that are similar to the European Directive 95/46/EC.[67]

Canadian law presents, for that reason, a useful case study for jurisdictions outside the EU and the US, as considerations about its speech and privacy norms are likely to be closer to those of many others. Moreover, Canada combines common law and civil law jurisdictions, which often take different approaches to protecting individual interests as a matter of private law. Adding the Canadian case study into the more frequent US-EU conversation can therefore be useful across legal systems, as the Canadian analysis of the RTBF may hold lessons for a wide number of jurisdictions that are considering creating their own version of the right, as the right continues to be considered in courts and legislatures globally.[68]

---

65 Franz-Stefan Gady, "EU/U.S. Approaches to Data Privacy and the 'Brussels Effects': A Comparative Analysis" (2014) 15 Georgetown J of Intl Affairs 12; James Q. Whitman, "The Two Western Cultures of Privacy: Dignity versus Liberty" (2004) 113:6 Yale LJ 1152 at 1160–1161.

66 Voss & Castets-Renard, *supra* note 10 at 313.

67 Eloise Gratton & Julien Polonetsky, "Droit a l'oubli: Canadian Perspective on the Global Right to be Forgotten Debate" (2016) 15:2 Colorado Tech LJ 337 at 339.

68 These include Argentina, Brazil, Colombia, India, Japan, and Korea. See DLA Piper, "Japan: Supreme Court Rules on the 'Right to be Forgotten'", *Privacy Matters* (14 February 2017); Yulchon LLC, "South Korea: Korea Communications Commission Releases Guidelines On 'The Right To Be Forgotten'", *Mondaq: Connecting Knowledge and People* (19 January 2017); Di Blasi, Parente, e Associados, "A Twist on the Brazilian Right to be Forgotten", *Lexology* (31 May 2018); Amber Siha, "Right to be Forgotten: A Tale of Two Judgements", *The Centre for Internet and Society* (7 April 2017); Valentina Manrique Gómez, "El Derecho al Olvido: Análisis Comparativo de las Fuentes Internacionales con la Regulación Colombiana" (2015) Revista de Derecho Comunicaciones y Nuevas Tecnologías at 9; Edward L. Carter, "Argentina's Right to be Forgotten" (2013) 27:1 Emory Intl L Rev 23; Vinod Sreeharsha, "Google and Yahoo Win Appeal in Argentine Case", *New York Times* (19 August 2010); Deepti Pandey, "The Right to be Forgotten: A Trail of Controversy and Conflict", *Indian Journal of Law and Technology* (18 March 2019); Shaikh Zoaib Saleem, "What is the right to be forgotten in India", *liveMINT* (14 August 2018). The US, while discussing it, has so far rejected the right. See John W. Dowdell, "An American Right to Be Forgotten" (2017) 52:2 Tulsa Law Review 311 at 331–332.

Finally, privacy law is by its very nature extraterritorial.[69] National privacy laws are applied extraterritorially by courts more than any other body of law because the sources and perpetrators of online harms are routinely in a different jurisdiction than their victim, so data protection regulations would be ineffective if they did not provide some protection from them. For example, based on such argument, a Canadian federal court held in *Globe24h* that a Romanian website that republished and indexed tribunal decisions breached PIPEDA and ordered it to refrain from the activity.[70] In the 2018 *Equustek* decision,[71] the Supreme Court of Canada ordered Google to delist on a global level a website that was selling stolen trade secrets. Although it did not refer to the RTBF *per se* since the plaintiff was a company and not an individual whose privacy had been violated, the case shows the willingness of the Court to force intermediaries to remove content on a global basis.[72] Therefore, and as the last chapter also shows by relating the book's content to international law, the book also provides considerations that can be applied globally, and provides a new perspective on a right that continues to be debated worldwide.[73]

## 5 This book

### 5.1 Common themes

This book is the first to address the RTBF in Canada. It does so by putting together a collection of essays by diverse scholars in the field of Canadian privacy law. The collection explores the evolution of the RTBF, its challenges, and impacts on privacy, reputation, and online speech.

Each chapter analyzes questions that legal actors and policymakers must consider as they move forward in shaping this new right: How does the RTBF fit into existing legal frameworks? How can Canadian courts and policymakers reconcile rights to privacy and rights to access to information and free speech?

---

69  See e.g. GDPR, recital 3, and arts 3(1), 3(2)(a).
70  *A.T. v Globe24h.com*, 2017 FC 114.
71  *Google Inc v Equustek Solutions Inc*, [2017] 1 SCR 824.
72  More recently, however, the extraterritoriality of privacy law found its limit. In the 2019, the ECJ limited the RTBF's territorial scope in the EU holding that the GDPR does not require search engines to delist on a global basis. See *Google LLC v. CNIL*, C-507/17, [2019] EUR-Lex CELEX No 62017CJ0507.
73  See Ignacio N. Cofone and Catalina Turriago Betancourt, "The Right to Be Forgotten in Peace Processes" (Chapter 6) for more details.

The chapters share a number of common themes. First, at a descriptive level, they engage with the position of the Office of the Privacy Commissioner of Canada that the RTBF is already present in Canadian privacy law because PIPEDA applies to search engines. This stance is consistent with the right's history (Stoddart) but raises issues of free speech (Scassa), Charter-compliance (Slane), and implementation (Deziel). They also indicate how Canadian privacy law is currently ill-equipped to address the complex issues posed by the RTBF. Second, at a normative level, they address the consequences of this insufficiency, and propose balancing approaches in the application of different versions of the RTBF to address online harms while keeping negative social consequences at bay. Third, they highlight in different ways that an underlying issue brought to light by RTBF is the power imbalances that exist between individuals and information services – and how current privacy laws (and consumer protection law) fail to provide proper remedies. In Scassa's chapter, this imbalance takes the shape of information asymmetries. In Slane's, it is about the way online profiling services have the power to define how employers, governments, and others view an individual without being held accountable under accuracy principles. In Deziel's, it is about the individual's consent and the way information is first collected through technologies that can be argued to be opaque and abusive. In Turriago Betancourt's and mine, it is about individuals' position in society and the two sides of public interest.

The chapters set the stage for the Canadian debate on the RTBF. They introduce the current state of the law and analyze the application of the right through the lenses of private law and constitutional law. Each chapter speaks to the main tensions in the implementation of the RTBF: privacy rights versus the right to access information and free speech. They consider the scope of these rights, and what their legal construction would mean for the introduction of the RTBF.

## 5.2 Roadmap

The rest of the book proceeds as follows.

In Chapter 2, Jennifer Stoddart notes that the RTBF has a long history in different legal traditions that precedes the 2014 *Google Spain* decision. This chapter traces that history and illustrates how components of the concept referred to as the RTBF are already present in many jurisdictions, particularly in French and UK law, which underpin the two Canadian legal traditions of common and civil law. Stoddart explores the "droit a l'oubli" in French law, and traces the recent history of the RTBF since the 2014 decision. While tracing historical versions of the RTBF across legal traditions, this chapter also brings forth the tensions at play in the debate to recognize a RTBF in the Canadian context – the balance between privacy and free speech. In doing so, it sets the stage for the chapters that follow.

In Chapter 3, Teresa Scassa argues that a ruling that PIPEDA applies to internet search engines raises significant free speech issues for individuals and risks exacerbating expanding information asymmetries between individuals and companies. Scassa considers the possibility of implementing the RTBF within the existing Canadian legal framework and raises the most critical issues in terms of balancing competing interests. Scassa explains how PIPEDA and provincial counterparts have tackled a balance between privacy and free speech in different ways. In a time of growing information asymmetries between citizens and states and citizens and corporations, speech and access to information are of crucial importance. The implementation of the RTBF requires a more comprehensive consideration of what its limits should be to ensure that free speech, including the right to access information often derived from speech rights, is not violated. She argues that speech includes individual autonomy and self-actualization through an individual's ability to collect information about others in their lives and communities, to process it, and communicate it. Private sector privacy legislation in Canada has approached this issue in different ways, including with the journalistic and personal use exceptions available in PIPEDA. The presence of these exceptions indicates that there is some protection for speech and individual autonomy in collecting and disclosing information that should be considered against the individual interest in privacy. Despite these exceptions, the law currently does not have the robust balancing framework that de-indexing would require, especially since de-indexing risks changing how ordinary internet users can collect information, in a world where individuals are already disadvantaged in terms of information compared to companies and the government.

In Chapter 4, Andrea Slane proposes how the RTBF can be reconciled with access to information by regulating information flows with a focus on privacy harms. Slane considers the application of the RTBF in online profiling and builds on Stoddart's chapter to discuss the evolution of delisting since *Google Spain* and the evolution of interests at the core of the RTBF in the Canadian context. Whether PIPEDA applies to search engines, the chapter argues, should be seen through the question of whether PIPEDA affords data subjects an avenue to enforce data protection principles on the services that deliver online profiling. She suggests that the question of whether PIPEDA affords individuals a RTBF should be considered with a view to a search engine's name search function, and not to the search engine more broadly. A search engine's name search function – which compiles and ranks information available online about that individual – should amount to this practice being viewed as an online profiling service. Casting the debate in this way refocuses on what PIPEDA is meant to address: online privacy harms. She explains that this idea better aligns with the harm that proponents of implementing the RTBF in PIPEDA seek to remedy – to ensure principles of accuracy in the results of individual name searches and avoid disclosure of inaccurate, irrelevant, and outdated information. Moreover, Slane engages with the free speech argument in Scassa's chapter and argues that, if the debate is narrowed to regulating online profiling, Charter-compliance should not be a problem for the RTBF, similarly to how free speech is not a problem for consumer reporting legislation.

In Chapter 5, Pierre-Luc Déziel argues that while the romantic ambitions of the RTBF are laudable and desirable, its implementation must be more than romantic. The debate over the RTBF in Canada points to larger issues such as power imbalances, free speech, and the utility of the consent model in privacy law, which need to be addressed on their own terms. To achieve its goal, defendants of the RTBF may have to be more radical, turn to new and drastic ways of reforming Canadian privacy law, and develop legal tools that are better suited for the era of global access to big data. Deziel argues that the main objectives of the RTBF can be implemented through the introduction of Privacy by Design (PbD) in Canadian privacy law and the incorporation of existing consumer protection models. The introduction of PbD could tackle issues such as design practices that regulate access to sensible data and vulnerabilities that stem from power imbalances between users of technologies and service providers. This chapter provides a way to move the discussion on the objectives of the RTBF forward. It builds on Scassa and Slane's work by suggesting that the RTBF with its romantic ambitions may not find the easiest fit in Canadian law. However, the issues the RTBF debate raises – which Scassa and Slane have elaborated on as well – point to larger structural issues in Canadian privacy law.

In Chapter 6, Catalina Turriago Betancourt and I take the debate to the international context. We propose for the first time that the RTBF can be applied in peace processes to facilitate their objectives of reconciliation. We build on Chapter 2 by analyzing the origins of the RTBF through a novel theoretical lens, focusing on transitions from conflict to peace. The 2014 *Google Spain* decision, combined with the history and forms of the RTBF in different jurisdictions, particularly in criminal law, also serves as a basis on which to develop a RTBF that is suitable to peace processes by reconciling the different rights in conflict. We engage with Scassa and Slane's arguments about reputational harms to individuals caused by online information about them, focusing on how reputational harms can impede reconciliation within peace processes, and describe the tension between privacy, victims' rights particular to transitional justice contexts, access to information, and expression rights. Building on Deziel's argument that the RTBF is a call to return to a state where information about individuals was not saved in systems of perfect memory that jeopardize reputation, we suggest that peace processes may benefit from considering delisting particular types of information about amnestied individuals.

# 2 Lost in translation

Transposing the right to be forgotten
from different legal systems

*Jennifer Stoddart*[*]

## 1 Introduction

In the five years since the European Court of Justice (ECJ) decision *Google Spain* (2014),[1] there has been an explosion of reactions and commentaries in the world of European-based law, particularly in the intellectual worlds of common-law heritage and, within that, especially from North American legal critics.[2]

The debate has been an impassioned one, as reference is quickly made to freedom of expression and the alleged consequences of any alteration to the conditions of application of this fundamental right.

Journalists and media interests, especially in North America, have been quick to mobilize, attempting to counter the threat of leakage of this concept, alleged to be inimical to liberty, outside the European Union.[3]

Leaving aside the very important and more recent question of how to determine the limits, if any, of the application of judgments made by national courts concerning information posted to the Internet, I will rely on my own experience as a law student many years ago to suggest that the current debate on the right to be forgotten is an important

---

[*] The author would like to express her thanks to Nicolas Charest and Julie Uzan-Naulin of Fasken for their assistance in the research. All opinions expressed here are her own and do not reflect the point of view of any person connected with Fasken.
1 Google Spain SL and Google Inc v Agencia Espanola de Proteccion de Datas (AEPD) and Mario Costeja Gonzalez, C-131/12, [2014] ECR I-317 [Google Spain].
2 See Amy Gajda, "Privacy, Press, and the Right to be Forgotten in the United States" (2018) 93:201 Wash L Rev, 201.
3 See generally Montreal Gazette Editorial, "Editorial: Is There a 'Right to be Forgotten'?" (30 May 2014), online: Montreal Gazette, https://montrealgazette.com/opinion/editorials/editorial-is-there-a-right-to-be-forgotten; Pierre Trudel, "Effacer le passé: un droit?" (7 July 2018), online: Le Devoir, https://www.ledevoir.com/opinion/chroniques/532531/effacer-le-passe-un-droit.

phase of the cross-fertilization of legal systems in the age of global information exchange.[4]

The 2014 right to be forgotten judgment appeared in continental European societies familiar with a concept, inherited from Roman law, that was part of their legal fabric. It also landed in common-law societies, particularly the United States, where legal culture held that freedom of expression was one of their defining characteristics. The stage was set for a collision.

However, many of the shock waves which have been generated by this debate may stem from a misunderstanding of what the right to be forgotten implies in civil law.

## 2 The right to be forgotten in French law

In a 1980 course at the McGill University Faculty of Law entitled *Procédure criminelle avancée* [*Advanced criminal procedure*], a distinguished criminalist, Michel Proulx, who later became a Quebec Court of Appeal justice, introduced his students to *"le droit à l'oubli"* in French law. Of course, we had not yet heard of it in our basic criminal law course. To the best of my recollection, he described it as a way for society to let people get on with their lives, once they had been punished and made amends, and thus to rehabilitate themselves. The right to be forgotten allowed a person to apply to the government to have the record of their misdeed effaced and accordingly start anew.

As I remember, this right to an administrative clean slate was presented in the part of the criminal procedure course that dealt with pardons in Canadian criminal law. In a similar fashion, law students learned, Canadians with a criminal record could apply for and receive, under certain conditions, a pardon from the Crown which included the removal of the notation of their criminal conviction from official records.

Interestingly, at about the same time, an amendment to the *Quebec Charter of Rights and Freedoms* was made to reinforce the legally neutral status of those whose criminal offence had been pardoned. It reads:

> *18.2. No one may dismiss, refuse to hire or otherwise penalize a person in his employment owing to the mere fact that he was convicted of a penal or criminal offence, if the offence was in no way connected with the employment or if the person has obtained a pardon for the offence.*[5]

---

4 See Google Inc v Equustek Solutions Inc, 2017 SCC 34, [2017] 1 SCR 824; See also Google LLC v Equustek Solutions Inc, Case No. 5:17-cv-04207-EJD (ND Cal 2017); Equustek Solutions Inc v Jack, 2018 BCSC 610, 2018 CarswellBC 911.

5 Charter of Human Rights and Freedoms, CQLR c C-12, s 18.2.

Similarly, French jurists refer to "*...la grande loi de l'oubli, cet élément si puissant de la vie des individus et des peuples...*" [*the great law of forgetting, this so powerful component of the lifes of individuals and peoples*][6] Thus, the underlying notion of the right to be forgotten is linked, in these legal traditions, to the expiry of prescription deadlines after which accusations for alleged penal code infractions may no longer be brought against individuals by the state.[7]

## 3 What exactly does the European Court of Justice say?

There are a number of different concepts that underlie the often-casual reference to the right to be forgotten. Facts are important in this debate.[8] The first case to attract widespread comment concerned Mr. Costeja Gonzalez, an individual who had had property sold at auction in 1998 for repayment of social security debts owed to the Spanish state. Some 12 years later, he was concerned to find that by using a search engine, the practical obscurity of newspaper records was now shattered. Well displayed at the top of the search result was the mention of his past behavior, casting a reputational shadow on his current self.

The ECJ in *Google Spain* (2014) ruled that European data protection law and the fundamental right to privacy justified a request to the search engine to remove the link between Mr. Costeja Gonzalez' name and the newspaper articles in question.[9] The right to be forgotten is mentioned only twice in this landmark judgment, when the Court refers to the arguments of the complainant Mr. Costeja Gonzalez and those of the Spanish and Italian governments. It is referred to in italics, as a subset of the rights to data protection and privacy to the extent, notably, that personal data shall be "fairly and lawfully processed", "collected for specified, explicit and legitimate purposes and are not further processed in a way incompatible with those purposes", "adequate, relevant and not excessive in relation to the purposes for which they are collected and/or further processed", and, beyond that

---

6 See Roger Merle et André Vitu, Traité de droit criminel: procédure pénale, 8th ed (Paris: Édition Cujas, 2000) at 66 quoted in Papa Keyi Abel Ndong, "Infléchissement du droit à l'oubli et cohérence de la procédure pénale de traitement du délit de blanchiment de capitaux" (2017) BDE 2 at 6.

7 See generally Rehabilitation of Offenders Act 1974 (UK), c 53.

8 See Karl Delwaide & Antoine Guilmain, "The 'Right to be Forgotten' has a three-piece suit tailor-made in Canada? From Quebec to British Columbia" (2017) 14 CPLR 157. (The authors point out that the right to be forgotten has been dealt with by Canadian courts in several contexts and in different ways.)

9 See Google Spain, *supra* note 1 at para 99.

"accurate and, if necessary, kept up to date."[10] If one of these conditions is not met, the right to be forgotten shall apply.

Often overlooked is the fact that the *Google Spain* case law does not implement a whole right to be forgotten. The right to dereferencing does not mean the deletion of information from the source website: the content can still be consulted by going directly to the original site.

An uproar of disbelief greeted this decision at the time. Commentators from the other side of the Atlantic found limiting freedom of expression in the name of an unfamiliar right, that to be forgotten was a dangerous inroad on democratic freedom. At the least, it was, said one critic, foggy thinking.[11]

However, the European Union continued on its path and adopted the General Data Protection Regulation in May 2016.[12] Article 17 and Recital 65 provide that a data subject should have the right to be forgotten where the retention of such data infringes this Regulation or Union or Member State law to which the data controller is subject.[13]

Since then, another important fact which has emerged is that search engines seem to have found a way to deal with requests for dereferencing. Subsequently, Google reported having recorded requests to delist some 2.4 million URLs between 2014 and 2017. Only 43% of them

---

10  Ibid at para 72.
11  See generally Steven C. Bennett, "The Right to Be Forgotten: Reconciling EU and US Perspectives" (2012) 30:1 Berkeley J Int 161.
12  See generally Michael L. Rustad & Sanna Kulevska, "Reconceptualizing the Right to Be Forgotten to Enable Transatlantic Data Flow" (2015) 28:2 Harv JL & Tech 349.
13  See EC, Regulation 2016/679 of April 27 2016 on the protection of natural persons to the processing of personal data and on the free movement of such data, and repealing Directive 95/46/EC (General Data Protection Regulation), [2016] OJ, L 119/1 at 65. Recital 65 states in part: [...] In particular, a data subject should have the right to have their personal data erased and no longer processed where the personal data are no longer necessary in relation to the purposes for which they are collected or otherwise processed, where a data subject has withdrawn their consent or objects to the processing of their personal data, or where the processing of their personal data does not otherwise comply with this Regulation. [...] However, the further retention of personal data should be lawful where it is necessary, for exercising the right of freedom of expression and information, for compliance with a legal obligation, for the performance of a task carried out in the public interest or in the exercise of official authority vested in the controller, on the grounds of public interest in the area of public health, for archiving purposes in the public interest, scientific or historical research purposes or statistical purposes, or for the establishment, exercise or defense of legal claims.

were, in fact, delisted. Some 89% of the requests came from private individuals and the rest from a combination of minors, corporate entities, politicians, and celebrities.[14]

Since 2014, the European legal system has continued to refine the definition of the circumstances giving rise to the right to be forgotten. The European Court of Human Rights (ECHR) found in 2018 that the German Supreme Court had correctly applied the balancing test relating to right to be forgotten claims involving two German individuals convicted for murder who, while released on probation in 2007, sought the removal of articles and the transcript of a radio station report about the murder from the website archives. Although the Court analyzed extensively the ECJ's *Google Spain* case law, the ECHR's finding is based solely on Article 8 of the European Convention on Human Rights, which provides for a broad right to privacy. More specifically, the ECHR court refused the request, deciding in this case that the right to privacy weighed less in the context than rights to freedom of expression and access to information.

Interestingly, the court acknowledged the important role of internet archives:

> *The availability of internet archives contributes greatly to the preservation and to the accessibility of new information. Digital archives constitute a precious source for teaching and for historical research in particular because they are immediately accessible to the public and generally provided free of charge.*[15]

One commentator noted nevertheless about this decision "*...the Court mentioned that internet websites can have a higher impact on individual privacy rights than traditional print media, and that search engines can contribute to an amplification effect.*"[16] Even a decade before, the

---

14 See Michee Smith, "Updating our 'Right to be Forgotten' Transparency Report" (26 February 2018), online: Google, https://blog.google/around-the-globe/google-europe/updating-our-right-be-forgotten-transparency-report/. See also Yann Padova, "Le Droit à l'oubli, un droit universel?" (2016) 130 Revue Lamy droit de l'immatériel 34. (The author raises numerous questions about the effects of the extra-territorial application of dereferencing or the right to be forgotten, notably the role of search engines in evaluating the requests of complainants.)
15 See ML and WW v Germany, No. 60798/10 and 65599/10 (28 June 2018). See also Robert Bolton, "The Right to Be Forgotten: Forced Amnesia in a Technological Age" (2015) 31:2 J Marshall J Info Tech & Privacy L 133.
16 See Winston Maxwell, "Top Human Rights Court Denies Right to be Forgotten in Old Murder Case" (21 August 2018), online: Chronicle of Data Protection,

Ontario Court of Appeal had found that cyber-libel incurs greater damage due to the nature of the internet as *"instantaneous, seamless, interactive, blunt, borderless and far-reaching."*[17]

## 4  Proceedings in Canadian courts

The origin of the right to be forgotten in continental penal law has dropped from attention in its current reincarnation as the numerical right to be forgotten in the data protection context. The recognition of this numerical right is, of course, of great interest to just about anyone who uses the internet today. But do the principles applicable in the penal context work for the right to be forgotten at large? Authors Delwaide and Guilmain summed it up succinctly:

> Can the right to be forgotten find application in the Canadian context and, if so, how? That was one of the questions posed in 2016 by the Office of the Privacy Commissioner of Canada in its Notice of consultation on online reputation.[18] Some 28 stakeholders (individuals, organizations universities, defence groups, etc.) participated in the consultation and 17 briefs expressed a position on the "right to be forgotten" in Canada. The end result: 10 against, four neutral, three in favour (including one concerning the specific case of children). One can already sense Canadians' reticence regarding the "right to be forgotten."[19]

And at the same time, apprehension that opening the door in Canadian law to the dereferencing of links used by search engines will be a significant limit on the important value of freedom of expression is a real

https://www.hldataprotection.com/2018/08/articles/international-eu-privacy/top-human-rights-court-denies-right-to-be-forgotten-in-old-murder-case/#page=1. See also Franz Werro, "The Right to Inform v. the Right to be Forgotten: A Transatlantic Clash" in Aurelia C. Ciacchi et al. (eds), Liability in the Third Millennium (Baden-Baden, FRG: Nomos, 2009) 285; Samuel D. Warren & Louis D. Brandeis, "The Right to Privacy" (1890) 4:5 Harv L Rev 193.

17  Barrick Gold Corporation v Lopehandia et al., [2004] OJ No 2329, 239 DLR (4th) 577 at para 31.

18  See generally OPC, "Notice of consultation on online reputation" (21 January 2016), online: Office of the Privacy Commissioner of Canada, https://www.priv.gc.ca/en/about-the-opc/what-we-do/consultations/consultation-on-online-reputation/or_consultation/.

19  Delwaide & Guilmain, *supra* note 7 at 1.

concern for many, voiced by Canadian media and the search engine, Google.[20]

The tensions at play are evidenced in the decision of the Prothonotary of the Federal Court in the reference of the Privacy Commissioner of Canada.[21] A motion had been brought by the Canadian Broadcasting Company and a group of Canada's largest media organizations, acting together, to be added as parties or, alternatively, given leave to intervene in the reference.

The two questions referred to the Federal Court by the Commissioner can be resumed as follows: (1) are Google research results characterized as commercial activities; and (2) if so, does the journalistic and literary exception apply to exempt them from the application of Personal Information Protection and Electronic Documents Act (PIPEDA)? In her decision, the Prothonotary wrote:

> *It is not disputed that the underlying complaint raises important and ground-breaking issues relating to online reputation, including whether a 'right to be forgotten' should be recognized in Canada, and if so, how such a right can be balanced with the Charter protected rights to freedom of expression and freedom of the press.*[22]

However, she rejected the motion, pointing out that at that early stage it was premature to leap to the conclusion that the Court would decide that the Privacy Commissioner can indeed investigate, that the journalistic or literary exemption did not apply to search engines, that the Privacy Commissioner would conclude that dereferencing is necessary, and that Google would follow his conclusion, which in any case would have no force of law. In addition, the obtention of an eventual order by the Federal Court would necessitate a de novo hearing.[23]

20 See generally Michael Geist, "Why a Canadian Right to be Forgotten Creates More Problems Than It Solves" (January 26 2018), online: The Globe and Mail, https://www.theglobeandmail.com/report-on-business/rob-commentary/why-a-canadian-right-to-be-forgotten-creates-more-problems-than-it-solves/article37757704/; Zachary Graves, "The Dangerous Proliferation of the 'Right to Be Forgotten'" (18 August 2014), online: Huffington Post, https://www.huffpost.com/entry/the-dangerous-proliferati_b_5507477.

21 See Reference re subsection 18.3(1) of the Federal Courts Act, RSC 1985, c F-7, 2019 FC 261 [Reference] at para 3.

22 Reference, *supra* note 20 at para 7.

23 See also Teresa Scassa, "Right to Be Forgotten Reference to Federal Court Attracts Media Concern" (17 April 2019), online: Teresa Scassa, http://www.teresascassa.ca/index.php?option=com_k2&view=itemlist&task=user&id=63%3Ateresascassa&limitstart=10.

A subsequent motion by Google to strike the reference of the Privacy Commissioner was also dismissed.[24] In rejecting the motion, the Prothonotary referred to these arguments:

> *[40] ... Google has characterized the grounds it raises as follows: first, that deciding the reference without addressing the inextricably intertwined constitutional issues is legally untenable because it would fail to put an end to the substantive dispute as to whether using PIPEDA to effectively censor Internet search engines is constitutional, and result in litigation by instalment; and second, that the proposed reference amounts to an abuse of process, and unduly and unfairly truncates and undermines Google's substantive and procedural rights.*

Undeterred, Google filed a notice of motion to have the Federal Court set aside the Prothonotary's order and recognize that Google was indeed entitled to raise the "...inextricably intertwined constitutional issues..." as part of the reference questions to be submitted to the Federal Court.[25] The basic argument is that PIPEDA restricts the constitutionally protected value of freedom of expression if it is found to apply to Google characterized as a search engine, affecting not only the search engine itself but also content creators such as news media.

## 5 Conclusion

This debate will foreseeably carry on for several years through different levels of adjudication. And the final conclusion will inevitably influence the drafting of the next generation of Canadian data protection law.[26]

The civil law concept of an individual's right to move on, once social atonement has been made or the information on them serves no justifiable social purpose, is arguably akin to the common law approach to pardon for criminal offences. But the notion of obtaining a social pardon seems to be eclipsed by the debate on freedom of expression.

24  See Reference re subsection 18.3(1) of the Federal Courts Act, RSC 1985 c F-7, 2019 FC 957 (CanLII) at para 40.

25  Ibid.

26  See IC, "Canada's Digital Charter: Trust in a Digital World" (25 June 2019), online: Innovation Canada, https://www.ic.gc.ca/eic/site/062.nsf/eng/h_00107.html.

The effects on the information flow of search engines and social media have brought both positive and negative consequences to our societies. The courts will need to use a careful, nuanced, and composite approach in determining appropriate rules for their scope and use in the future.

# 3 A little knowledge is a dangerous thing?

## Information asymmetries and the right to be forgotten

*Teresa Scassa*

## 1 Introduction

People like to control what others know or think about them. From deciding what clothes to wear to deciding who to hang out with or even what cell phone to own, individuals make daily choices about the image they present to the world. This image may shift or change over time – a person might choose to "remake" themselves as they move from one social group to another or as their views or ideas evolve. In some cases, people are embarrassed by their former selves – horrifying haircuts, poor choices of partners, embarrassing antics, cringe-worthy life choices, or even criminal transgressions. Before the internet, it was much easier to escape past versions of ourselves; today, however, the past easily haunts us through seemingly indelible online images, ill-judged posts, and even news reports.

The risks and consequences of having our identities shaped by out-dated, inaccurate or even just plain embarrassing online personal information are such that the protection of online reputation has become a compelling issue for Canadians. The risks are even more significant for young Canadians who have spent their entire lives as digital citizens, and who may be forced to deal not just with an internet history of poor adolescent decision-making, but also with images and anecdotes posted by friends or family members – often without their knowledge or consent.

The "right to be forgotten" (RTBF) is seen by some as necessary to redress the most problematic consequences of past peccadillos. It is linked to privacy in two ways. One is through a kind of right to obscurity – to be invisible to others, at least to some extent, if one chooses. The other is through the ability to control what is known about oneself. This is a reputational dimension of privacy that is more commonly protected in European countries – and in Québec.[1] The RTBF has become a major and evolving issue in Europe, where data protection and privacy laws treat privacy as a human right. It is an emerging issue in Canada – one that is both presently before the courts and likely to be part of some future reform of the *Personal Information Protection and Electronic Documents Act* (PIPEDA).[2]

This chapter urges caution in approaching a RTBF in Canada. While recognizing that the problem of rogue information is devastating for some, there are important rights at stake besides privacy that must be taken into account. The Privacy Commissioner's reference to the Federal Court on whether PIPEDA in its current incarnation applies to the search functions of search engines has raised the potential for privacy complaints that focus on de-indexing as a means of obscuring certain personal information online. The freedom of expression implications for the media and for those who host or share online information are likely to be vigorously argued in court. But the informational interests of ordinary individuals in an age of growing information asymmetry may be less clearly advanced. These include the rights of individuals to discover information and to communicate it. As appropriate recourses develop around the most egregious and non-consensual forms of online information such as revenge porn, it is necessary to consider whether a RTBF is needed under PIPEDA, and if so, how its limits should be carefully crafted.[3]

## 2 The emergence of the right to be forgotten in Europe

The "right to be forgotten" in relation to search engines traces its origins to a 2014 decision of the European Court of Justice. In *Google Spain SL, Google Inc. v Agencia Española de Protección de Datos,*

---

1 For example, art. 3 of the *Civil Code of Quebec*, CQLR c CCQ-1991, groups together reputational and privacy rights: "3. Every person is the holder of personality rights, such as the right to life, the right to the inviolability and integrity of his person, and the right to the respect of his name, reputation and privacy."

2 *Personal Information Protection and Electronic Documents Act*, SC 2000, c 5 [PIPEDA].

3 See, for example, *Intimate Images and Cyber-protection Act*, NS Reg 101/2018, c 7; *The Intimate Image Protection Act*, CCSM c I87; *Protecting Victims of Non-consensual Distribution of Intimate Images Act*, RSA 2017, c P-26.9; *Intimate Images Protection Act*, RSNL 2018, c I-22.

*Mario Costeja González*,[4] the complainant sought to have information that had been published in an online version of a newspaper in
1998 de-indexed from Google's search engine. He objected to the fact
that information about the forced sale of his property was returned
in searches of his name online, arguing that Google's search algorithms persisted in linking his name to information about him that
he considered no longer to be relevant. The European Court of Justice
confirmed that search engine companies engaged in the processing of
personal information when generating search results of the kind objected to by the complainant. The Court recognized that a data subject
had a right to request erasure of personal data in some circumstances,
including where information returned in search results was "inadequate, irrelevant or excessive in relation to the purposes of the processing, that they are not kept up to date, or that they are kept for
longer than is necessary."[5] The removal of the data from search results
by search engine operators is achieved by the de-indexing of the pages
on which the information is found.

*Costeja* was decided prior to the coming into effect of the General
Data Protection Regulation (GDPR) which expressly includes a right
to erasure.[6] This right requires a data controller to erase personal data
about an individual at that individual's request in specified circumstances; the right is also balanced with competing rights and interests,
including the freedom of expression. Of course, the right to erasure
is broader than de-indexing. The right to erasure is tied to the right
to withdraw consent to the continued use and disclosure of personal
information to which a person might at one point have consented. The
RTBF is different. Often the information sought to be de-indexed is
present not because the individual chose to share it, but because it was
published in news reports, court decisions, or other communications
that are independently protected by the freedom of expression.

4 *Google Spain SL and Google Inc v Agencia Espanola de Proteccion de Datas (AEPD)
and Mario Costeja Gonzalez*, C-131/12, [2014] ECR I-317.
5 Ibid at para 92.
6 See generally EC, *REGULATION (EU) 2016/679 OF THE EUROPEAN PARLIA-
MENT AND OF THE COUNCIL of 27 April 2016 on the protection of natural persons
with regard to the processing of personal data and on the free movement of such data,
and repealing Directive 95/46/EC (General Data Protection Regulation)*, [2016] OJ,
L 119/1; EC, *Corrigendum to Regulation (EU) 2016/679 of the European Parliament
and of the Council of 27 April 2016 on the protection of natural persons with regard to
the processing of personal data and on the free movement of such data, and repealing
Directive 95/46/EC (General Data Protection Regulation)*, [2018] OJ, L 127/1.

## 3 The Canadian context

Although PIPEDA has been referred to as "quasi-constitutional" in status,[7] it does not frame privacy as a fundamental human right. Rather, it creates a balance between an individual's "right to privacy" and the need of organizations to collect, use, and disclose personal information. PIPEDA is silent as to any specific RTBF. There are limits on data retention,[8] and organizations are required to ensure that information they hold about a person is "as accurate, complete, and up-to-date as is necessary for the purposes for which it is to be used."[9] Yet in many cases, what people seek to have forgotten *is* accurate – it is just embarrassing, was published without the individual's consent, or is no longer part of the identity a person wishes to share with the world. Some work is required therefore, to even build the argument that the specific right is found within the law. This is separate and apart from the question of whether the law applies to search engine functions, or whether it is capable of shaping the appropriate balancing of values that would be required if it did.

The question of whether existing data protection law in Canada includes a RTBF was considered in *CL c BCF Avocats d'affaires*.[10] The Commission d'accès à l'information du Québec assessed a complaint in which the complainant sought to have her name disassociated from a company that had once employed her. Because she had virtually no other web presence, search engines tended to return search results that linked her to her former place of employment, even though her former employer had removed her information from their active web site. The adjudicator found that her former employer had met its requirements under the accuracy principle by removing her information. It had no obligation to take further steps to ensure that Google de-indexed links between her name and versions of its site stored in internet archives. The adjudicator stated that the accuracy principle was not the equivalent of a RTBF and expressed doubt that such a right existed in Quebec.

---

7 See e.g. *Eastmond v Canadian Pacific Railway*, 2004 FC 852 at para 100, 2004 CarswellNat 1842; *Nammo v TransUnion of Canada Inc*, 2010 FC 1284 at para 75, 2010 CarswellNat 4908 (note that there is no free-standing right to privacy in the Canadian Constitution; the nearest thing is a right to be free from unreasonable search or seizure in s. 8 of the *Canadian Charter of Rights and Freedoms*, The Constitution Act, 1982, Schedule B to the Canada Act 1982 (UK), 1982, c 11).

8 See PIPEDA, *supra* note 2, c 4.5 of Schedule I (provides that personal information should be retained only as long as necessary for the fulfillment of the stated purposes for collection).

9 Ibid., c 4.6 of Schedule I.

10 2016 QCCAI 114.

PIPEDA and its provincial legislative counterparts must also strike a balance between protecting privacy and ensuring the freedom of expression.[11] Each of Canada's private sector data protection laws walks the privacy/freedom of expression line in a variety of ways. One of these is to exempt from their scope, the collection, use, or disclosure of personal information for journalistic, literary, or artistic purposes.[12] While PIPEDA and the Personal Information Protection Acts (PIPAs) in Alberta and British Columbia[13] do this by excluding the application of the law to information collected, used, or disclosed for journalistic purposes "and for no other purpose," Quebec's law takes a somewhat different approach. It does not apply to information collected, used, or disclosed for "the legitimate information of the public."[14] Not only does this avoid the uncomfortable need to define "journalism" in the age of the internet, but it also retains some role for the privacy commissioner by requiring a consideration of whether more personal information was published than was necessary for the "legitimate information of the public." While the trend elsewhere in Canada has simply been to determine if something was published for journalistic purposes and no other purpose, and then to set it outside the scope of review, in Quebec, the commissioner has reviewed even content in the mainstream press to see if the details reported went beyond what was necessary for the public to be legitimately informed about an issue.[15]

Another important aspect of data protection laws that balances privacy and the freedom of expression is the exclusion from review of personal information that is collected, used, or disclosed by individuals for purely personal or domestic purposes.[16] Under PIPEDA this has been interpreted to give a broad latitude to individuals in their

11 See generally *Alberta (Information and Privacy Commissioner) v United Food and Commercial Workers, Local 401*, 2013 SCC 62, [2013] 3 SCR 733.
12 See Teresa Scassa, *"Journalistic Purposes and Private Sector Data Protection Legislation: Blogs, Tweets, and Information Maps"* (2010) 35 *Queen's LJ* 733.
13 See *Personal Information Protection Act*, SA 2003, c P-6.5; *Personal Information Protection Act*, SBC 2003, c 63.
14 *Act respecting the protection of personal information in the private sector*, CQLR c P-39.1, s 1.
15 See e.g. *Valiquette c Gazette*, 1996 CarswellQue 1156, [1997] RJQ 30 (the Quebec Court of Appeal ruled that the plaintiff's right to privacy was violated by news reports that a teacher with AIDS was being paid full salary even though he was not teaching. The teacher in question was the plaintiff, and the story had been written in such a way as to make him identifiable. While there was a public interest in the information at the heart of the story, the way in which it had been communicated did not adequately respect the individual's right to privacy).
16 PIPEDA, *supra* note 2, s 4(2)(*b*).

need to seek out and use the personal information of others. This exception is important, and its freedom of expression dimensions have perhaps been lost in the assumption that it primarily draws a line between commercial activity (to which PIPEDA applies) and noncommercial activity (to which it does not). Cases that have interpreted this exception have tended to treat it as walking this line. For example, in *Ferenczy v. MCI Medical Clinics*,[17] the court ruled that personal information collected by a private investigator on behalf of an insurance company was not collected in the course of "commercial activity." Applying principles of agency, the court found that had the physician/defendant used his own video camera to record the evidence, it would have been exempt from PIPEDA because it was collected for purely personal or domestic purposes. Thus, a person employed by him to capture the same information for the same purposes – in this case a private investigator – should be able to benefit from the same exception. Justice Dawson noted: "The defendant through his representatives was employing and paying an investigator, to collect information for him. It is the defendant's purpose and intended use of the information that one should have regard to in determining the applicability of the Act."[18] Similarly, in *State Farm Mutual Automobile Insurance Company v. Privacy Commissioner of Canada*,[19] the Federal Court found that collecting evidence to defend oneself in a law suit was not "commercial activity," and that it did not become commercial activity when a private investigator or a law firm is retained by an individual to gather information on his or her behalf.[20] In such circumstances, the actions of the organization are those of the individual; they are personal and not commercial.

Yet although both *Ferenczy* and *State Farm* focus on the distinction between personal and commercial activity to determine PIPEDA's application, and while PIPEDA depends upon the existence of commercial activity for its constitutional validity, it is important not to lose sight of the other reason for excluding from PIPEDA's application the collection, use, or disclosure of personal information for purely personal reasons. To be free, autonomous, and self-actualizing, individuals must be able to find, process, communicate, and share information about one another – and they must be able to do so largely without interference from the state. While concerns over freedom of

---

17  2004 CarswellOnt 1706, [2004] OJ No. 1775.
18  Ibid at para. 30.
19  2010 FC 736, 2010 CarswellNat 2225.
20  Ibid at para 106.

expression and data protection law have been focused largely on the "journalistic purposes" and the "literary or artistic purposes" exceptions, the exception for purely personal purposes is also fundamental to freedom of expression. There is an intense human rights dimension to an individual's ability to gather information about those around them, to process it, to communicate it, and to use it in different ways. It is fundamental to a person's development, liberty, and well-being. It is also a communal value. This is what it means to live in a community and a society. While gossip may be harmful and malicious, there are plenty of communications of personal information that are meant to inform, to warn, to reassure, or to build bonds between individuals.

In a smaller community and in simpler times, people had ways to acquire the information they needed about what was going on in the lives of those around them – and perhaps, more importantly, to know who might be untrustworthy, abusive, dishonest, or given to malice or cruelty. These channels still exist in small communities; in our towns and cities, though, apart from close personal networks, people have become increasingly dependent upon the internet for information about those they encounter. The internet is a place in which people share a sometimes-astonishing amount of personal information about themselves. It is also a place where they go to learn about others.

Of course, the internet is used by many people for many purposes, which complicates approaches to the RTBF. It is now common to hear stories of employers who have used search engines to find information about job applicants; and about landlords who look up potential tenants, to give just two examples. Social media posts have been used in police investigations, and are frequently used in civil litigation.[21] Past mistakes could become barriers to such fundamentally important things such as employment and shelter. Privacy commissioners generally warn employers that the information they find online about prospective employees may be inaccurate, out-of-date, or even malicious.[22] Even so, the fact that unfavorable information or images

---

21  See e.g. *Leduc v Roman*, 2009 CanLII 6838, [2009] OJ No 681; *Schuster v Royal & Sun Alliance Insurance Co of Canada*, 2009 CanLII 58971, [2009] OJ No 4518. See also *Sparks v Dubé*, 2011 NBQB 040, 2011 CarswellNB 80; *Stewart v Kempster*, 2012 ONSC 7236, 2012 CarswellOnt 16567; *Conrod v Caverley*, 2014 NSSC 35, 2014 CarswellNS 49; *Isacov v Schwartzberg*, 2018 ONSC 5933, 2018 CarswellOnt 16828.

22  See e.g. OPC, "Privacy and Social Networking in the Workplace" (December 2015), online: *Office of the Privacy Commissioner of Canada*, https://www.priv.gc.ca/en/privacy-topics/privacy-at-work/02_05_d_41_sn/; OIPC BC, "Conducting Social Media Background Checks" (May 2017), online: *Office of the Information & Privacy Commissioner for British Columbia*, https://www.oipc.bc.ca/guidance-documents/1454.

may be found is a risk for job-seekers. The RTBF offers an end-run around this type of snooping – it would allow individuals to seek the de-indexing of some content – to obscure if not remove it – so that it becomes effectively erased from their past.

## 4 The Commissioner's position

In 2017, the Privacy Commissioner of Canada initiated a consultation on digital reputation. In the ensuing report,[23] Commissioner Therrien indicated that he was of the view that PIPEDA, in its unamended form, applied to the search functions of search engines, which were therefore obliged to comply with PIPEDA in relation to those functions. The Commissioner expressed the desire "to create an environment where individuals may use the internet to explore their interests and develop as persons without fear that their digital trace will lead to unfair treatment."[24]

The Commissioner's position is that when a person enters the name of a neighbor or co-worker into a search engine and the search engine returns a list of results, the search engine has collected, used, and/or disclosed this information in the course of commercial activity and PIPEDA therefore applies. PIPEDA requires an organization to maintain accurate, complete, and up-to-date information. According to the Commissioner, an individual could leverage this principle to require the de-indexing of a site. However, the "accuracy" requirement in PIPEDA is that "Personal information shall be as accurate, complete, and up-to-date as is necessary for the purposes for which it is to be used." It is important to note that the RTBF is not simply or even primarily about correcting misinformation – in many cases it is about avoiding past embarrassments. The information is not inaccurate – it is simply something the individual no longer wants to have shaping perceptions of them. The accuracy obligation is therefore an awkward place to locate the RTBF. It is important to note that de-indexing does not require the search engine to actually remove the content – something it could not do, since the content is hosted by another organization. Rather, it means that the search engine would

23 OPC, "Draft OPC Position on Online Reputation" (26 January 2018), online: *Office of the Privacy Commissioner of Canada*, https://www.priv.gc.ca/en/about-the-opc/what-we-do/consultations/consultation-on-online-reputation/pos_or_201801/ [*Online Reputation*].
24 Ibid.

have to take steps to ensure that the content does not appear in search results for the affected individual.

Many of those who made submissions to the Commissioner during the consultation process raised doubts about whether such a system could work.[25] They also expressed concerns about the potential impact on freedom of expression – and indeed, a right of this kind would have to be balanced with that freedom.[26] The Commissioner acknowledged the need to balance the RTBF with freedom of expression; in the *Report on Online Reputation*, he indicated that "this balance can best be achieved in the context of online reputation by considering whether the accessibility of personal information is in the public interest."[27] In his view, "where there is a sufficient public interest in the information remaining accessible, this will normally trump an individual's desire to control access to their personal information that has been lawfully published online."[28] The challenge lies, of course, in assessing the public interest in any given circumstances – and anticipating what it might be in the future.

25 See e.g. Joe Bricker et al., "Response to the Notice of Consultation and Call for Essays — Online Reputation" (August 2016), online: *Office of the Privacy Commissioner of Canada*, https://www.priv.gc.ca/en/about-the-opc/what-we-do/consultations/consultation-on-online-reputation/submissions-received-for-the-consultation-on-online-reputation/or/sub_or_10/; Google Canada, "Can the right to be forgotten find application in the Canadian context and, if so, how?" (August 2016), online: *Office of the Privacy Commissioner of Canada*, https://www.priv.gc.ca/en/about-the-opc/what-we-do/consultations/consultation-on-online-reputation/submissions-received-for-the-consultation-on-online-reputation/or/sub_or_19/; Eloïse Gratton and Jules Polonetsky, "Privacy Above All Other Fundamental Rights? Challenges with the Implementation of a Right to Be Forgotten in Canada" (August 2016), online: *Office of the Privacy Commissioner of Canada* https://www.priv.gc.ca/en/about-the-opc/what-we-do/consultations/consultation-on-online-reputation/submissions-received-for-the-consultation-on-online-reputation/or/sub_or_03/.
26 See e.g. BC Freedom of Information and Privacy Association, "Submission to Consultation on Online Reputation (FIPA)" (August 2016), online: *Office of the Privacy Commissioner of Canada*, https://www.priv.gc.ca/en/about-the-opc/what-we-do/consultations/consultation-on-online-reputation/submissions-received-for-the-consultation-on-online-reputation/or/sub_or_13/; The Globe and Mail, "Submission to the OPC's Consultation on Online Reputation (Globe and Mail)" (August 2016), online: *Office of the Privacy Commissioner of Canada*, https://www.priv.gc.ca/en/about-the-opc/what-we-do/consultations/consultation-on-online-reputation/submissions-received-for-the-consultation-on-online-reputation/or/sub_or_22/.
27 *Online Reputation, supra* note 23.
28 Ibid.

On October 10, 2018,[29] the Commissioner launched a reference to the Federal Court on the issue of the RTBF. The reference is linked to a complaint filed against Google with the Office of the Privacy Commissioner (OPC) by an individual. The complainant is concerned that Google searches of his name produce links to news articles that he alleges "are outdated and inaccurate and disclose sensitive information such as his sexual orientation and a serious medical condition."[30] The complainant's view is that by providing prominent links to these articles, Google is breaching PIPEDA. He is seeking to have these results de-indexed. The articles would not be taken down, but they would not appear in Google search results using his name. Unless similar orders were made against other search engines such as Bing, the content would still be findable.

The Commissioner has referred two questions to the Federal Court. First, he seeks to know whether Google's search engine activities constitute the "commercial activity" necessary to bring these activities within the scope of PIPEDA, which applies to the collection, use, or disclosure of personal information in the course of commercial activity. The second question is whether Google's search engine activities, even if commercial, fall within the exception to PIPEDA's application where personal information is collected, used, or disclosed "for journalistic, artistic or literary purposes and for no other purpose."[31] Google has since challenged the scope of the reference. It seeks to add the question of whether, if PIPEDA does apply to the search engine's activities, and if there is a de-indexing order, such an order would violate s. 2(*b*) of the *Canadian Charter of Rights and Freedoms*.[32]

## 5  The right to be forgotten and the freedom of expression

It is evident that the RTBF clashes directly with the freedom of expression. It does so in two different ways. In the first place, de-indexing ensures the relative obscurity of certain content. In this sense, it limits the expressive rights of the publisher of the content – by ensuring

---

29 See OPC, "Privacy Commissioner Seeks Federal Court Determination on Key Issue for Canadians' online reputation", (10 October 2018), online: *Office of the Privacy Commissioner of Canada*, https://www.priv.gc.ca/en/opc-news/news-and-announcements/2018/an_181010/.

30 *Reference re subsection 18.3(1) of the Federal Courts Act, RSC 1985, c F-7*, 2019 FC 261 at para 6.

31 PIPEDA, *supra* note 2, s 4(2)(*c*).

32 This motion to expand the scope of the reference had not yet been heard.

that it will no longer be easily found using the principal tool by which content is discoverable in today's world. However, it also limits the freedom of expression of the searcher – the freedom of expression is widely considered to include the liberty to inform oneself. It is not surprising, then, that media outlets have sought to vigorously oppose the federal Privacy Commissioner's reference to the Federal Court.[33]

There are also serious problems with the application of PIPEDA to the activities of search engines. In large part, a search engine is merely the agent of the searcher who is the party that will be using the information. If the searcher is a private person searching for personal reasons, PIPEDA simply does not – or should not – apply. If the searcher is an organization engaged in commercial activity, the search engine is not privy to the purposes for which the information is to be used, and is not in a position to make that sort of determination.

The agency relationship is part of the logic of cases such as *State Farm* and *Ferenczy*. These cases address the sphere of private information gathering – something that is at the heart of individual freedom of expression, as well as individual autonomy. There is even a dimension of privacy here – at least for the individual who is engaged in searching for information and who should generally not be interfered with by government in their quest for information. Although the Commissioner seeks to make Google (or other search engines) accountable, the end result is that ordinary users become unable to access information they are seeking.

It is the very ordinariness of these individuals that is crucially important here. We live in an age of profound information disparity and disequilibrium. Vast quantities of personal information are collected by the state and by organizations in the private sector alike, and we are profiled and surveilled to an unsurpassed extent. On the flip side, internet giants are manipulating the information we receive through targeted advertisement, targeted feeds, and content; even our search results are customized to our user profiles. We are already information-challenged.

Make no mistake, when major corporations or the government seek to know more about any of us, they do not put our names in internet search engines and browse through the results. Detailed profiles and analytics – incorporating information from a broad array of public and private sources – are prepared in-house, or are available to anyone

---

33 Reference, *supra* note 30.

who has the resources to pay.[34] For state actors and large corporations there are massive, inscrutable, and omniscient data sources. By contrast, for the mother wanting to see if someone offering in-home child care is an appropriate choice, for the woman seeking to ensure that the person she is dating is not a creep or a liar, for the person who is concerned that his employer may be directing latent homophobia towards him, there are search engines.[35] De-indexing of internet content will change what ordinary individuals are able to know about other people; it will not change what corporations or governments are able to know. This is why, apart from all of the other complexities of implementing a RTBF and of balancing it with freedom of expression and other values, we need to tread very carefully. Information asymmetries are very real and very harmful. We should avoid making them worse.

PIPEDA, a statute crafted for a simpler age of data collection, use, and disclosure, has significant and well-documented shortcomings when it comes to our contemporary information society and economy. Much ink has already been spilled – by critics, legal scholars, courts, current and former Commissioners, and by Parliamentarians – outlining the deficiencies in the law. The Minister of Innovation, Science and Economic Development has recently issued a discussion paper on PIPEDA reform that makes it clear that updating the law is a priority.[36] On the RTBF, though, the document is evasive – observing that the matter is before the courts. This is a bit of a cop-out. One of the problems with the Commissioner's attempt to squeeze the RTBF into the current version of PIPEDA is that the law entirely lacks any kind of framework for navigating the complex balancing of rights and interests that will need to be achieved if de-indexing is to become routine. In any event, the Minister of Innovation, Science and Economic

---

34  See generally OPC, *Data Brokers: A Look at the Canadian and American Landscape: Report Prepared by the Research Group of the Office of the Privacy Commissioner of Canada* (Quebec: Office of the Privacy Commissioner of Canada, 2014).

35  A study of de-indexing requests in Europe following the *Costeja* decision indicated that a significant number of requesters seek to de-index content related to their legal history. The authors of the study recount instances where individuals convicted of crimes including domestic violence and fraud sought to have links to information about these convictions de-indexed even though the de-indexing criteria were not met. See Theo Bertram et al., "Three years of the Right to be Forgotten" at 7, online: https://elie.net/static/files/three-years-of-the-right-to-be-forgotten/three-years-of-the-right-to-be-forgotten-paper.pdf.

36  IC, "Strengthening Privacy for the Digital Age" (21 May 2019), online: *Innovation, Science and Economic Development Canada*, https://www.ic.gc.ca/eic/site/062.nsf/eng/h_00107.html.

Development has also announced a *Digital Charter* designed to set out the principles that will guide the development of law and policy in the digital age.[37] Control over personal information is a pillar of this Charter: "Canadians will have control over what data they are sharing, who is using their personal data and for what purposes, and know that their privacy is protected." This does not really get to the heart of the issues with the RTBF. It is notable as well that nothing in the *Digital Charter* addresses the freedom of expression (other than to reference certain limits on hateful and violent speech).

That the RTBF requires some careful thought and framing is evident. Data provided by both Google and Bing following the *Costeja* decision make evident the number of requests to de-index online content.[38] After the initial burst of requests following the 2015 decision, the number of de-indexing requests has settled into an average of 45,000 per month in European countries.[39] A study on three years of de-indexing data by researchers affiliated with Google noted that 33% of de-indexing requests related to social media and 20% related to information were found on news or government websites. They also found that a majority of requests related to the requester's history with the law.[40] The researchers noted that most requests came from private individuals (as opposed to celebrities, politicians, and other public figures), and that only 43% of them met the criteria set for de-indexing.

## 6 Conclusion

In Canada, search engines already can and do de-index search results in some circumstances – usually where there is a court order. These court orders may be grounded in other statutory regimes that address speech that falls outside accepted boundaries, including a proliferation of new laws addressing the non-consensual posting of intimate images online.[41] These laws tackle the most egregious instances of

---

37  IC, "Canada's Digital Charter: Trust in a Digital World" (25 June 2019), online: *Innovation, Science and Economic Development Canada*, https://www.ic.gc.ca/eic/site/062.nsf/eng/h_00108.html.

38  See Google Transparency Report, "Requests to Delist Content under European Privacy Law" (30 May 2019), online: *Google Transparency Report*, https://transparencyreport.google.com/eu-privacy/overview?hl=en; Microsoft, "Content Removal Requests Report", online: *Microsoft*, https://www.microsoft.com/en-us/corporate-responsibility/crrr.

39  See Bertram et al., *supra* note 35 at 5.

40  Ibid.

41  See e.g. CCSM c I87; RSA 2017, c P-26.9; NS Reg 101/2018, *supra* note 2.

online information that can haunt individuals and destroy their lives and peace of mind. There may be other categories of information in which de-listing is appropriate, and no doubt, the Commissioner's approach to PIPEDA is intended to capture other forms of unwanted online content. However, the problems with opening the door wide to complaints about online content are manifold. Even if only the most egregious circumstances result in orders of erasure, the potential to divert scarce Privacy Commissioner resources into dealing with complaints aimed at limiting what individuals can see online (and yet having no impact whatsoever on the ability of the state and corporations to surveil and profile us) seems a dangerous misdirection of resources. Even if the burden of dealing with complaints is shifted to search engines, there is a risk that search engines could be swamped with de-indexing requests. This could lead to potentially uneven and problematic compliance, and could overburden an important research resource relied upon by almost everyone.

# 4 Reconciling privacy and expression rights by regulating profile compilation services

*Andrea Slane*

## 1 Introduction

When a search service aggregates information connected to a person's name from online sources, it produces the most straightforward and easily accessible composite of that person's online identity. This online profile, consisting of content that may or may not be authored by the subject, has become a central component of our social and professional lives.[1] To counteract the risks of inaccurate, incorrect, or outdated information playing a disproportionately prominent role in a person's online identity, privacy and data protection regimes must be adapted to face the changing technological and social conditions under which these profiles are compiled and delivered to the public. The "right to be forgotten" – more specifically, the application of data protection principles to services that compile a profile of an individual from publicly available materials online – provides a means to mitigate the negative impact that distorted online profiles can have.[2] With the explosion of data collection from so many different public and semi-public online channels, appropriately administered data protection principles can bolster our otherwise greatly diminished capacity to meaningfully address problems with information that is circulating about us online.[3]

1  See generally Alice E. Marwick, *Status Update: Celebrity, Publicity and Branding in the Social Media Age* (New Haven: Yale University Press, 2013). ISBN: 978-0-300-19915-4.
2  See Ganaele Langlois & Andrea Slane, "Economies of Reputation: The Case of Revenge Porn" (2017) 14:2 Comm & Crit/Cult Stud 120. doi:10.1080/14791420.2016. 1273534.
3  See Norberto Nuno Gomes de Andrade, *"Oblivion: The Right to be Different ... from Oneself: Re-proposing the Right to Be Forgotten"* in Alessia Ghezzi, Angela Guimarães Pereira and Lucia Vesnić-Alujević, eds, *The Ethics of Memory in a Digital Age: Interrogating the Right to Be Forgotten* (London, UK: Palgrave Macmillan, 2014). ISBN 978-1-137-42845-5.

Granting data subjects an avenue for regaining some measure of control over at least the most straightforward violations of personal data protection principles – namely, accuracy, which includes correctness and currency – is necessary to address the vast power imbalances between data subjects and digital information brokers, including information location service providers, such as search engines.[45]

The Court of Justice of the European Union (CJEU) famously initiated the current call for applying data protection principles to search engines in the landmark case of *Google Spain, SL, Google Inc v Agencia Española de Protección de Datos (AEPD), Mario Costeja* [*Google Spain*], where the Court considered the specific role that search engines play in processing personal data when a person's name is searched.[6] The CJEU considered search engines to both greatly facilitate access to information about a data subject and to compile a profile from otherwise disparate online sources.[7] As the CJEU describes it, people who enter a person's name as a search term obtain "through the list of results a structured overview of the information relating to that individual that can be found on the Internet enabling them to establish a more or less detailed profile of the data subject."[8] The Court found that the unique effect of this compiled list of results is potentially greater than any one result contained on the list, because the list as a whole:

> ...potentially concerns a vast number of aspects of [one's] private life and which, without the search engine, could not have been interconnected or could have been only with great difficulty — and thereby to establish a more or less detailed profile of [the subject]. Furthermore, the effect of the interference with those rights of the data subject is heightened on account of the important role played by the internet and search engines in modern society, which render the information contained in such a list of results ubiquitous.[9]

---

4  See generally OPC, "Draft OPC Position on Online Reputation" (26 January 2018), online: *Office of the Privacy Commissioner of Canada*, https://www.priv.gc.ca/en/about-the-opc/what-we-do/consultations/consultation-on-online-reputation/pos_or_201801/ [*Draft OPC Position*]; See also Teresa Scassa, "A Little Knowledge Is a Dangerous Thing?: Information Asymmetries and the Right to Be Forgotten" (Chapter 3).

5  See Julia Powles, "The Case That Won't Be Forgotten" (2015) 47 Loy U Chicago LJ 583 at 586.

6  See *Google Spain SL Google Inc v Agencia Española de Protección de Datos (AEPD) and Mario Costeja González*, C-131/12, [2014] ECR I-317 [*Google Spain*].

7  Ibid at paras 36 and 37.

8  Ibid at para 37.

9  Ibid at para 80.

In Canada, the very live question of whether the *Personal Information Protection and Electronic Documents Act* (PIPEDA) applies to search engines should in my view be seen specifically through the question of whether PIPEDA should afford data subjects an avenue for enforcing the accuracy principle on services that deliver such *profiles*.[10] To cast the debate about the "right to be forgotten" more broadly, and especially to consider the freedom of expression analysis more broadly as a question of users' rights to access information through search engines, would be to lose sight of what it is that the application of PIPEDA is meant to address in this context: namely, to provide a remedy for a particular type of online privacy harm arising from distorted profiles compiled from online sources.

## 2  Unstable specificity: applying PIPEDA to search engines

The Office of the Privacy Commissioner (OPC) has taken the position, albeit so far only in a draft position paper on online reputation (*Draft OPC Position*), that PIPEDA should be interpreted to obligate search engines to abide by fair information principles in relation to searches of a person's name.[11] The *Draft OPC Position* names de-indexing as one of two "key mechanisms for enhancing one's control over their online reputation," where de-indexing is described as "the process by which a webpage, image or other online resource is removed from search engine results when an individual's name is entered as a search term."[12] The OPC refers to Google's own characterization of its goal as to "provide people with access to relevant information from the most reliable sources available"[13] and so concludes that, "with respect to searches for an individual's name, search engines use personal (and non-personal) information to create a dynamic profile of what they consider to be the most 'relevant' information available online which is available to be indexed in relation to that individual."[14]

10 See generally *Personal Information Protection and Electronic Documents Act*, SC 2000, c 5 [PIPEDA].
11 See *Draft OPC Position*, *supra* note 4.
12 Ibid.
13 *Draft OPC Position* referencing Ben Gomes (VP Engineering for Google), "Our Latest Quality Improvements for Search" (25 April 2017), online: *Google* https://www.blog.google/products/search/our-latest-quality-improvements-search/.
14 *Draft OPC Position*, *supra* note 4.

While the OPC has rightly suggested that it would be unreasonable to require search engines to abide by PIPEDA as a whole, in particular with regard to securing advance consent for its collection and use of personal information, there are nonetheless significant ways that central data protection principles in PIPEDA, especially the accuracy principle, can be applied in a justifiable, rights-balancing way.[15] As the OPC puts it, "search engines should, thus, be *responsive to challenges* that the profile presented in the form of search results is not accurate, complete, or up-to-date" (emphasis added), and should on a case-by-case basis determine whether de-indexing or some other response "such as lowering the ranking of a result, or flagging it as inaccurate or incomplete" is appropriate.[16] Throughout the report, the OPC acknowledges the central task of striking a balance between the need for individuals to have some avenue to correct inaccurate profiles and freedom of expression, where the determination of how to resolve the complaint "should take into account the public interest in the information remaining accessible."[17] As Teresa Scassa notes in this volume, "The challenge lies, of course, in assessing the public interest in any given circumstances – and anticipating what it might be in the future."[18] While balancing of privacy with the public interest in personal information remaining readily accessible will not always be easy, other areas of law (such as privacy torts, access to information requests) as well as the European experience post *Google Spain* indicate that such balancing is by no means impossible.

Despite the OPC's specifying what it proposes to accomplish by applying PIPEDA narrowly to complaints related to search engine results of a person's name, the OPC has filed a reference in the Federal Court regarding the more general question of whether PIPEDA applies to search engines at all: (1) whether Google's search engine service collects, uses, or discloses personal information in the course of commercial activities, and (2) whether Google is exempt because its purposes are exclusively journalistic or literary.[19] These questions

---

15 See *Draft OPC Position, supra* note 4; See also PIPEDA, *supra* note 10 at 4.6 (The accuracy principle is set out *"Personal information shall be as accurate, complete, and up-to-date as is necessary for the purposes for which it is to be used"*).
16 *Draft OPC Position, supra* note 4.
17 Ibid.
18 Scassa, *supra* note 4.
19 OPC, "Announcement: Privacy Commissioner Seeks Federal Court Determination on Key Issue for Canadians' online reputation" (10 October 2018), online: *Office of the Privacy Commissioner of Canada*, https://www.priv.gc.ca/en/opc-news/news-and announcements/2018/an_181010/.

arise, as do all issues pertaining to the OPC's authority over private sector data protection, from the specific wording and interpretation of PIPEDA,[20] and are a response to Google's initial rejection of the OPC's assertion of any jurisdiction over Google's search services.[21] Stating the reference questions as set out in the legislation may be necessary to address the issue of authority more generally, but it loses some of the crucial focus on name searches, whereby Google's service most specifically collects, uses, and discloses personal information of a particular person.

Perhaps recognizing that on strict statutory interpretation search services likely would be subject to PIPEDA, Google moved to be permitted to challenge the application of PIPEDA to search engines as a violation of s. 2(b) freedom of expression rights not justified under s. 1 of the *Charter of Rights and Freedoms* (*Charter*).[22] This motion was denied, Google appealed, and the Federal Court confirmed that the reference was not the appropriate proceeding in which to address a s. 2(b) challenge.[23] Google had claimed that applying PIPEDA to search engines grants the OPC "the power to censor otherwise lawful content existing on the Internet."[24]

However, when put into the perspective of the underlying more narrow application of PIPEDA, Google would be arguing that the *Charter* does not permit the state to require a company to respond to complaints about faulty information they have compiled into an

---

20  PIPEDA, *supra* note 4 s 4(1)(a) states that PIPEDA applies to "every organization in respect of personal information" that "the organization collects, uses or discloses in the course of commercial activities" and s. 4(2)(c) which sets out an exception to PIPEDA's application for "any organization in respect of personal information that the organization collects, uses or discloses for journalistic, artistic or literary purposes and does not collect, use or disclose for any other purpose."

21  See *Reference re subsection 18.3(1) of the Federal Courts Act, RSC 1985, c F-7*, 2019 FC 261 at para 8 (CanLII) [*Reference 18.3*] (concerned questions or issues of law and jurisdiction concerning the *Personal Information Protection and Electronic Documents Act*, SC 2000, c 5 that have arisen in the course of an investigation into a complaint before the Privacy Commissioner of Canada).

22  See *Canadian Charter of Rights and Freedoms*, s 7, Part I of the *Constitution Act, 1982*, being Schedule B to the *Canada Act 1982* (UK), 1982, c 11, s. 2(b) [*Charter*]; See also *In the Matter of a Reference Pursuant to Subsection 18.3(1) of the Federal Courts Act, RSC 1985, c F-7 of Questions and Issues of Law and Jurisdiction Concerning the Personal Information Protection and Electronic Documents Act, SC 2000, c 5 That Have Arisen in the Course of an Investigation into a Complaint Before the Privacy Commissioner of Canada*, 2019 FC 957 (CanLII) [*Google's Notice of Constitutional Question*].

23  Ibid.

24  Ibid at para 6.

online profile. To deny that PIPEDA applies to search engines at all affords too much leeway for businesses to compile personal information profiles, as if the online search service business model exempts the service provider from being subject to the principles and protections that have been established regarding offline information compilation and dissemination pertaining to a particular person. While there is no doubt that individuals use search services to legitimately find out information about other people, and that this activity falls within protected expression rights, it does not follow that s. 2(b) guarantees easy access to all information about a person.[25]

If we refocus the issue on whether PIPEDA should regulate services that provide aggregated online profiles of individuals, rather than whether de-indexing in general violates freedom of expression rights, then the affinities between what PIPEDA can do to support important consumer protection principles come back into line with the *Charter*.

## 3 PIPEDA as consumer protection against faulty profiles

The business of providing profiles of individuals has long been regulated as an aspect of consumer protection law, although enforcement of these rules in relation to online profiling businesses has sometimes been thwarted by issues of application, as elaborated below. Nonetheless, the affinities between the OPC's view of search engines as profile compilers and legislation regulating consumer reports are easy to spot. In the Draft OPC Position, the OPC suggests factors relevant to assessing the public interest in information remaining accessible, which should inform decisions about whether sites containing inaccurate personal information should be de-indexed, including:

- whether the individual concerned is a public figure (e.g. a public office holder, a politician, a prominent business person);
- whether the information at issue relates to a matter of public controversy or debate;
- whether the information relates to an individual's private life as opposed to, for example, their professional or working life;

---

25 For a more thorough discussion of the distinction between profile compilation and news reporting, for instance, see Andrea Slane, *"Search Engines and the Right to Be Forgotten: Squaring the Remedy with Canadian Values on Personal Information Flow"* (2018) 55:2 *Osgoode Hall LJ* 349.

- whether the information concerns a criminal offence for which the individual has been given a discharge, a pardon, or a record suspension; and,
- whether the information relates to a minor.[26]

These factors mirror those employed by Google in its fulfillment or denial of requests to de-index under European Union (EU) data protection law, following the *Google Spain* decision at the CJEU.[27] They also reflect similar requirements in legislation dealing with services compiling reports on consumers in Canada and elsewhere, which should provide some insight into how the *Charter* would not prohibit imposing accuracy requirements on a search engine's results list related to a person's name. Put more simply, well-established principles of accuracy in relation to consumer profiles should be upheld in relation to search engines for the same reasons they were established for consumer reporting offline. Information's "existing" on the internet does not absolve a search engine of its obligations to provide a remedy for data subjects adversely impacted by inaccurate or outdated information contained in a name search results list. While some commentators have argued that the rights of search engine users looking to locate information on a person should be paramount, this argument presumes that such a searcher's rights of access extend to inaccurate and outdated information, which is harder to justify.[28]

Regulation of businesses that compile personal information that is relevant to determining the character and financial credit-worthiness of consumers restricts the free flow of personal information, regardless of its public "existence." Provincial statutes govern this sort of business in Canada, for instance Ontario's *Consumer Reporting Act*[29] and British Columbia's *Business Practices and Consumer Protection Act*.[30] Other provinces have similar statutes.[31] These statutes place specific accuracy and relevance requirements on the information contained in

---

26  *Draft OPC Position, supra* note 4.
27  See generally Google Transparency Report, "Search Removals under European Privacy Law" (30 May 2019), online: *Google*, https://transparencyreport.google.com/eu-privacy/overview?hl=en [*Google Transparency Report*].
28  Scassa argues against de-indexing merely embarrassing rather than inaccurate information, which is a different category of information than what I am arguing falls within the consumer report type of information that more easily can be determined to be accurate or not. See Scassa, *supra* note 4.
29  Consumer Reporting Act, RSO 1990, c C 33 [CRA].
30  Business Practices and Consumer Protection Act, SBC 2004, c 2 [BPCPA].
31  See also Quebec's *Consumer Protection Act*, CQLR c P-40.1 [*CPA*].

such a report, although the legislation is often targeted to a regulated consumer reporting industry and so is more narrowly focused than PI-PEDA, namely focusing on businesses that provide profiles to clients that would extend credit, tenancy, insurance, or employment to the data subject.[32] The kind of personal information that is considered to comprise a consumer report includes personal information such as an individual's

> name, age, place of residence, previous places of residence, marital status, spouse's name and age, number of dependents, particulars of education or professional qualifications, place of employment, previous places of employment, estimated income, paying habits, outstanding debt obligations, cost of living, or obligations and assets.[33]

While this is an even more narrow band of information than what is potentially at issue in applying PIPEDA's accuracy principle to name search results, the structure of restrictions on this industry is a useful analogy.

Namely, obligations placed on consumer reporting businesses to maintain accuracy, currency, and relevance typically include general obligations to only include information based on "the most reliable sources reasonably available," as well as specific obligations not to include outdated information – usually prohibiting inclusion of adverse information beyond six or seven years after the resolution of the adverse circumstances (e.g. bankruptcy or other debt discharge; criminal conviction records after conviction, release, or parole). These restrictions consider this information to be outdated after that time and so no longer relevant to the individual's character and credit-worthiness, and instead merely prejudicial (there are some exceptions such as multiple bankruptcies). Further, the statutes forbid inclusion of personal information about criminal charges that did not result in conviction, or any conviction for which an absolute discharge has been granted or a pardon issued.[34] Here again, the fact of having been charged but not convicted, or otherwise excused of the criminal charges through discharge or pardon, means these events are not deemed to be relevant to the data subject's character or credit-worthiness. And so, despite the

32 *CRA, supra* note 29, s 8(1)(d); *BPCPA, supra* note 30, s 108(1)(a).
33 *BPCPA, supra* note 30, s 106; See also *CPA, supra* note 31, s 1(1).
34 See *BPCPA, supra* note 30, s 109 and *CRA, supra* note 29, s 9(3).

public availability of this information, it is not to be included in such a report. Importantly, all of these statutes provide a means for consumers to challenge the accuracy and completeness of any information contained in the report, and the business providing the report must, in the Ontario example, "correct, supplement or delete the information in accordance with good practice."[35]

The tricky part about the regulation of businesses that provide profiles of people compiled from public sources is that the statutes regulating consumer reports vary in terms of which businesses they apply to and how they make those distinctions. Ontario's statute, for instance, requires registration of a "consumer reporting agency" which is defined by way of the definition of "consumer report" which is, in turn, defined as providing credit or personal information "pertaining to a consumer for consideration in connection with a purpose set out" – namely, lending, tenancy, insurance, employment, and so forth.[36] In the United States, this same kind of circular definition in the federal *Fair Credit Reporting Act* (*FCRA*) has been shown to undermine the purpose of the Act with regard to some online profiling companies, since a business that disclaims providing reports for the designated purposes is then not a consumer reporting agency and is not required to abide by these restrictions, even if the disclaimer is entirely disingenuous.[37] Here is where Internet-based profile providers have thrown a wrench in the works of consumer protection by providing profiles to anyone for any purpose, just as Google further lumps searches of a person's name together with any other search, which they thus consider to exempt them from restrictions.[38]

---

35  *CRA, supra* note 29, s 13 (1).

36  Ibids 1(1); see also *BPCPA, supra,* s 106. BC has a broader and more encompassing definition that does not fall victim to this type of circularity, and so generally captures all entities that provide consumer reports which are simply defined as "written, oral or other communication respecting credit information of an individual" compiled for gain or profit, or on a routine non-profit basis "as an ancillary part of a business carried on for gain or profit." Presumably this could include a website that does not charge for reports, but gets its revenue from other means, like advertising or traffic direction.

37  *Fair Credit Reporting Act*, 15 USC § 1681 at § 603 [*FCRA*].

38  Thomas Daigle, "Europeans have a 'Right to be Forgotten' online. Should Canadians?" (26 Sept 2019), online: *Canadian Broadcasting Corporation News*, https://www.cbc.ca/news/technology/right-to-be-forgotten-canada-eu-court-1.5297528 ("Google maintains that de-listing represents a slippery slope. In a statement to CBC, the company said 'removing lawful information from a search engine limits access to media properties, past decisions by public figures and information about many other topics.' Peter Fleischer, Google's global privacy counsel,

An example of a failed effort to enforce the *FCRA* against an on-line profile provider was initiated by the Federal Trade Commission (FTC) against Spokeo Inc., a company that assembles consumer information from online and offline sources to create "consumer profiles" and sells access to these profiles to individuals or businesses via subscription.[39] According to Spokeo's FAQs, results may include "cell and landline phone numbers, email addresses, location history, family members, social media photos and social profiles, court records, historical records, and demographic data such as marital status and ethnicity."[40] In 2012, the FTC filed a complaint against Spokeo, Inc. for violations of the *FTC Act* and the *FCRA*, mainly because Spokeo had been specifically marketing its services to the human resources industry as means of background screening in hiring decisions.[41] Spokeo reached a settlement with the FTC in which Spokeo paid an $800,000 fine and ceased marketing to the HR industry.[42] However, Spokeo still offers exactly the same services and even continues to offer high volume "enterprise" subscriptions. It now merely repeats the following disclaimer on every page of its website: "Spokeo is not a consumer reporting agency as defined by the Fair Credit Reporting Act (FCRA). Do not use this site to make decisions about employment, tenant screening, or any purpose covered by the FCRA."[43] Spokeo thereby avoids the obligation to ensure accuracy, currency, or relevance of the information it offers up about an individual, leaving data subjects without recourse when inaccurate or outdated information is included in a report about them.

Absolving online profile providers of the requirement to provide a means for data subjects to correct inaccurate information has led to the rise of a business model where data subjects have been coerced into paying an often hefty fee in order to correct or remove

said freedom of expression is a 'broadly recognised – and passionately defended – right in Canada.' 'We believe that every Canadian has the right to access lawful information'").

39  See US, *Federal Trade Commission, United States v Spokeo, Inc* (CV12-05001) (2012) [*US v Spokeo*]; for more in-depth discussion of this case see Andrea Slane, "Information Brokers, Fairness, and Privacy in Publicly Accessible Information" (2018) 4:1 *Can J Contemporary & Comparative L* 249.

40  Spokeo, "What Results will I See When I Do a Search?" (30 May 2019), online: *Spokeo*, https://www.spokeo.com/enterprise.

41  See *US v Spokeo, supra* note 39; Leslie Fair, "Speaking of Spokeo: Part 1" (12 June 2012), online: *Federal Trade Commission*, https://www.ftc.gov/news-events/blogs/business-blog/2012/06/speaking-spokeo-part-1.

42  Ibid.

43  Spokeo, *supra* note 40.

inaccurate information (this same "fee-for-removal" scheme was also employed by shady businesses seeking to profit from removing illegally posted materials for a fee such as revenge porn).[44] Profiling sites that specialize in criminal arrest records, jail holding information, and especially mugshots have employed this business model, while disclaiming any obligation to ensure accuracy or to correct errors.[45] The most prominent of these sites, Mugshots.com, scrapes public records and compiles them into easy to access profiles associated with a person's name. As with Spokeo, Mugshots.com displays a warning not to use the site for *FCRA* purposes.[46] The site further prominently proclaims its shelter behind the First Amendment, claiming it does not need to correct errors or provide updates, since it merely reflects records as they existed in the sources from which they were taken (law enforcement, jail, court records).[47] The website's business model consists mostly of traffic direction to other search services (such as Truthfinder, a similar service to Spokeo): however, Mugshots.com previously employed a fee structure requiring a data subject to pay to have their information corrected, updated, or otherwise removed.[48] The operators of Mugshot.com were charged in May 2018 with extortion, money laundering, and identity theft in relation to this fee scheme.[49] The website subsequently discontinued charging data subjects to have their information updated or corrected (in other words, now a person can request updating and correction of their profile free of charge, if they can provide documents substantiating their claim). Mugshots.com subsequently dug in to their stance that

44  See Langlois & Slane, *supra* note 2; Andrea Slane & Ganaele Langlois, "Debunking the Myth of 'Not My Bad': Sexual Images, Consent and Online Host Responsibilities in Canada" (2018) 30:1 *CJWL* 42.
45  *Slane, Information Brokers, supra* note 39.
46  Mugshots, "Mugshots.com News" (30 May 2019), online: *Mugshots*, https://mugshots.com/.
47  Ibid.
48  Ibid (Older versions of the website are available through the Internet Archive: Wayback Machine, https://archive.org/web/).
49  See Jason Tashea, "Alleged owners of Mugshots.com Charged in Extortion Scheme, Face Extradition to California" (18 May 2018), online: *ABA Journal*, http://www.abajournal.com/news/article/alleged_owners_of_mugshots.com_arrested_extortion_scheme_face_extradition. The same type of fee structure has also been dismantled in relation to revenge porn, see also Slane & Langlois, *supra* note 44; Federal Trade Commission, "FTC, Nevada Obtain Order Permanently Shutting Down Revenge Porn Site MyEx" (22 June 2018), online: *Federal Trade Commission*, https://www.ftc.gov/news-events/press-releases/2018/06/ftc-nevada-obtain-order-permanently-shutting-down-revenge-porn.

they are merely reporting information as it exists in public online sources, however inaccurate it may be, by rebranding as "Mugshots. com News."[50]

Spokeo and Mugshots.com are examples of online profiling companies that take advantage of legal loopholes arising from legislation drafted well before the development of technologies that make it easy to scrape content from various online information sources, compile them, and then offer them immediately to any users looking for information on a particular person.[51] While search engines like Google are not specifically oriented toward providing online profiles to users, the search results returned upon search of a person's name similarly compile online information into a profile, and so when a search engine completes this particular type of search, the search engine is at that point similar to these explicit profile-providing businesses. To claim that because the underlying information "lawfully exists on the Internet" it is fair to include it in a profile without obligation to correct it when it is inaccurate or outdated – which is essentially what Google has argued – does not address the problems that inaccuracy, incompleteness, and outdatedness visit on the subjects of these profiles, and that consumer reporting obligations seek to remedy. The question is not whether the underlying information serves or has served the public interest in the abstract, but whether its continued *uncorrected* availability in search results related to an individual's name is in the public interest.

---

50 See Mugshots, *supra* note 46.
51 As Frank Pasquale wrote:

> [n]ew threats to reputation have seriously undermined the efficacy of health privacy law, credit reporting, and expungement. The common thread is automated, algorithmic arrangements of information, which could render a data point removed or obscured in one records system, and highly visible or dominant in other, more important ones ... [it] is not much good for an ex-convict to expunge his juvenile record, if the fact of his conviction is the top Google result for searches on his name for the rest of his life. Nor is the removal of a bankruptcy judgment from a credit report of much use to an individual if it influences lead generators' or social networks' assessments of creditworthiness, and would-be lenders are in some way privy to those or similar reputational reports.

Frank Pasquale, "Reforming the Law of Reputation" (2015) 47:2 Loy U Chicago LJ 515 at 516.

## 4 Conclusion: adapted application of PIPEDA to name search results

Returning to the issue at hand in Canada, the more precise question remains whether PIPEDA is going to be the means by which search engines will be obligated to respond to complaints about prominent name search results that contain inaccurate, incorrect, or outdated personal information, where the public interest does not weigh in favor of the ongoing availability of that information as associated with that person's name. As the earlier examples show, if the issue is considered in this more narrow way, then the *Charter* should not prohibit such a requirement, in the same way that it does not prohibit consumer reporting regulation, as these businesses also merely compile information from existing sources. If the application of PIPEDA is too broadly conceived – for instance, as applied to other types of searches beyond name searches – then the *Charter* analysis would have to consider a much stronger interference with access to expressive material, where the search engine's operation is not specifically tied to collection, use, and disclosure of personal information about an identifiable individual.

A different level of public interest in access will undoubtedly also apply to news stories about a person that might appear in name search results. But despite a lot of initial uproar about news articles disappearing from search results following *Google Spain* (with Google stoking the media into censorship outrage rather than aiming for more balanced responses),[52] Google has in the meantime implemented a workable means of deciding when to de-index and when not to de-index even news article results from name searches in the EU.[53] According to a recent study analyzing Google's decisions to de-index complaints, Google was found to only rarely de-index news stories, with roughly 5% of complaints received related to news sources and 81% of these complaints rejected.[54] Google has made distinctions based on which news items should remain associated with a person's name search – major crimes, for instance, and incidents involving breaches of trust or professional obligations. These sorts of guidelines should also be part

---

52 See Natasha Lomas, "Google Super Successful at Spinning Europe's Right to Be Forgotten as Farce" (4 July 2014), online: *Tech Crunch*, https://techcrunch.com/2014/07/04/digital-theatre/; *Google Transparency Report, supra* note 27.

53 See *Google Transparency Report, supra* note 27.

54 See generally Reputation VIP, "Forget.me: découvrez la réalité du droit à l'oubli" (31 May 2019), online: *Reputation VIP*, https://www.reputationvip.com/fr/blog/forget-me-fr.

of the OPC's determination of complaints in Canada, as suggested by the *Draft OPC Position*. Indeed, the Spanish Data Protection Authority that started the "right to be forgotten" ball rolling with the *Google Spain* decision subsequently denied a further request by the complainant to de-index a news article that discussed that decision. While the debt announcement underlying the original complaint was outdated and did not meet the threshold of a countervailing public interest in maintaining access to that information upon a name search, the more recent news stories about the CJEU case did meet that threshold, even if they also described the outdated information underlying the original claim.[55]

This sort of nuanced reasoning is appropriate in Canada as well and would ensure that fair information principles of accuracy are foregrounded but subject to the overarching PIPEDA reasonableness requirement, which includes consideration of the public interest in maintaining access to that information.[56] The OPC has clearly stated its position that PIPEDA should not be applied the same way to search engines as it is to other sorts of businesses, and its *Draft OPC Position* makes no reference to broader application of PIPEDA to search engines beyond the results associated with a name search. The Federal Court has stated that if PIPEDA is determined to apply to search engines, then the freedom of expression issues will depend on how it is applied.[57] Therefore, future s. 2(b) *Charter* challenges should not be determined in relation to the application of PIPEDA to search engines as a whole but should instead be assessed as they pertain to applying PIPEDA to search engines when they deliver particular search results associated with a person's name. The OPC will need to establish *Charter*-compliant guidelines for how to determine whether complaints are well-founded, which is undoubtedly a new task for the OPC. Guidance can be sought from the EU experience not only with the right to be forgotten but also with other means of

---

55  See Miquel Peguera, "No More Right-To-Be-Forgotten for Mr. Costeja, Says Spanish Data Protection Authority" (3 October 2015), online: *The Center for Internet and Society*, http://cyberlaw.stanford.edu/blog/2015/10/no-more-right-be-forgotten-mr-costeja-says-spanish-data-protection-authority.

56  See PIPEDA, *supra*, ss 3 and 5(3).

57  The Federal Court states that prior to a determination by the OPC on a complaint,

> there is no indication that PIPEDA, in any way, limits the operation of a search engine. At this time, no news article has been ordered delisted and it is speculative, at this stage, to assume that this will be the result of the investigation.

*Google's Notice of Constitutional Question, supra* note 22 at para 67.

making such determinations with regard to personal information flow in Canada (for instance, from criminal law, consumer protection law, and defamation law).[58] A narrow approach to applying the *Charter* to online profile compilation would be more in keeping with the actual aim of the "right to be forgotten" so far in contemplation in Canada and would help forge a more balanced path between privacy and expression rights to access information about others.

---

58  See Slane, *Search Engines, supra* note 25; Slane, *Information Brokers, supra* note 39. See also, Pierre-Luc Deziel, "Let's Not Dwell on the Past: The Right to be Forgotten as More than a Romantic Revolution" (Chapter 5). In his contribution to this volume, Pierre-Luc Deziel argues that "privacy law cannot deal with these issues on its own [...] privacy law in Canada might not only need to start looking ahead, but it should also look to its side."

# 5 Let's not dwell on the past

## The right to be forgotten as more than a romantic revolution

*Pierre-Luc Déziel*

## 1 Introduction

Induced by our increasing capabilities to generate, store, and retrieve information, the advent of a collective near perfect memory brings new concerns about people's privacy. Our ability to act and live in the present, to control our image and reputation, to let go of the past, and to start afresh are all challenged by this new and yet artificial power to collectively remember everything. The adoption in Europe of what is commonly referred to as the right to be forgotten (RTBF) is seen by many as an effective way to alleviate some of these concerns. Designed to allow people to control what others can "remember" about them, the RTBF sits on two core mechanisms: de-indexing and source takedown. De-indexing refers to the process by which informational location services delete from search results the links that are associated with queries of a person's name. Since the underlying content remains intact, and thus still available online, de-indexing is relatively limited in scope and may be better thought of as a right to obscurity.[1] Source takedown takes the RTBF further, because it allows data subjects to ask for the removal of their personal information directly at the source. This second component of the RTBF, which may be best described as a right to erasure,[2] provides stronger privacy protection but also presents important challenges to online freedom of speech.[3]

---

1 See Andrea Slane, "Search Engines and the Right to Be Forgotten: Squaring the Remedy with Canadian Values on Personal Information Flow" (2018) 55 Osgoode Hall LJ 349 at 358.
2 Ibid.
3 See OPC, "Draft OPC Position on Online Reputation" (26 January 2018), online: *Office of the Privacy Commissioner of Canada*, https://www.priv.gc.ca/en/about-the-opc/what-we-do/consultations/consultation-on-online-reputation/pos_or_201801/.

The RTBF is a play on memory. As Viktor Mayer-Schöenberger suggests, "remembering is a two-step process" that implies the transfer of information to long-term storage and the recall of that information from memory.[4] Each of the two core mechanisms of the RTBF has a role to play in that process. Source takedown erases information that is stored, and de-indexing limits the capacity to retrieve information that was committed to memory. If the RTBF's cardinal goals are to allow people to control what is actually remembered about them, to curate their image and reputation, and to let go of the past, then, I would argue, it falls short of addressing one fundamental point: how information about them is actually generated in the first place. For personal information to be stored in and retrieved from memory, it must already exist. While focusing on information that is already "out there," the current debate on the RTBF diverts our attention from the fact that the biggest threat to informational privacy is the automatic, spontaneous, and continuous generation and storage of information by the technologies that we use. Connected devices and mobile applications are deliberately designed to record a wide variety of sensitive information, such as GPS location, consumer-tracking data, Facebook "likes," or search entries, which nourishes the perfect memory the RTBF seeks to suppress.

It could be said, at this point, that other domains of privacy law are geared toward making our digital footprint leaner. Privacy by design (PbD)[5] comes to mind. PbD is indeed a more proactive approach to privacy, since it advocates for privacy protections to be embedded into the design and architecture of IT systems.[6] PbD is not a new idea,[7] but its introduction in the General Data Protection Regulation (GDPR)[8]

---

4 See Viktor Mayer-Schöenberger, *The Virtue of Forgetting in the Digital Age* (Princeton: Princeton University Press, 2009) at 17.

5 See EC, REGULATION (EU) 2016/679 OF THE EUROPEAN PARLIAMENT AND OF THE COUNCIL of 27 April 2016 on the protection of natural persons with regard to the processing of personal data and on the free movement of such data, and repealing Directive 95/46/EC (General Data Protection Regulation), [2016] OJ, L 119/1, art 25.

6 See Privacy by Design Centre of Excellence, "The Seven Foundational Principle" online: *Ryerson University*, https://www.ryerson.ca/pbdce/certification/seven-foundational-principles-of-privacy-by-design/.

7 Privacy by design has been developed by Ann Cavoukian, former Information and Privacy Commissioner of Ontario, in the early nineties to address systemic privacy risks of information and communication technology. See, Ann Cavoukian, "Privacy by Design. The 7 Foundational Principles" (January 2011), online: *Information and Privacy Commissioner of Ontario*, https://www.ipc.on.ca/wp-content/uploads/resources/7foundationalprinciples.pdf.

8 GDPR, *supra* note 5.

has strengthen its position has a valid approach to privacy. Despite the technical challenge of encoding privacy rules into algorithms,[9] promising and successful PbD initiatives have emerged in the last few years. Anonymity protocols and tools have been developed to secure payment and communication systems and artificial intelligence (AI) techniques, such as differential privacy and federated learning, have improved existing privacy enhancement technologies.[10][11] In Canada, for example, the Ontario and Gaming Corporation successfully applied biometric encryption technologies to facial recognition systems used for its "self-exclusion," which was implemented in 27 of its locations.[12]

The RTBF and the PbD approach are often thought of as addressing two distinct moments in the management of information flows: PbD focuses on data collection and generation, and the RTBF focuses on communication and access. However, contemporary technologies alter the traditional chronology of information flows and often blend distinct data processing phases into one operation.[13] In other words, the RTBF and PbD must not be thought of as two moments that are juxtaposed, but as two approaches that need to be superimposed within the same framework. The point of this short essay is simple. The core legal mechanisms of the RTBF – de-indexing and source takedown – are geared toward better control over personal information which is already generated, collected, shared, and accessible. In order to really address the privacy concerns and power imbalances that result from permanent memory, the RTBF should also focus on spontaneous data collection techniques and strategies that are embedded in the design of contemporary IT systems. The RTBF should not only be a right to obscurity and a right to suppression but also a right to not be documented in the first place. PbD and the RTBF should be two superimposed layers of a broader framework on which our laws should be grounded.

9 See e.g. Bert-Jaap Koops & Ronald Leenes, "Privacy Regulation Cannot Be Hardcoded. A Critical Comment on the 'Privacy by Design' Provision in Data-protection Law" (2011) 28:2 Intl Rev L Comp & Tech 159.
10 See Ira s. Rubinstein, "Regulating Privacy by Design" (2011) 26:3 BTLJ 1409 at 1415.
11 See also Andrea Scripa Els, "Artificial Intelligence as a Digital Privacy Protection" (2017) 31:1 Harv JL & Tech 217 at 220–222.
12 See Avner Levin, "Privacy by Design by Regulation: The Case Study of Ontario" (2018) 4:1 Can J of Comp & Contemporary L 115 at 129.
13 See Pierre-Luc Déziel, "Les limites du droit à la vie privée à l'ère de l'intelligence artificielle: groupes algorithmiques, contrôle individuel et cycle de traitement de l'information" (2018) 30:3 CPI 829 at 844.

## 2  Romanticizing the debate on the right to be forgotten

The RTBF is not yet explicitly recognized by Canadian privacy law. Following the decision of the Court of Justice of the European Union in *Google Spain v AEPD*[14] and the adoption of the GDPR by the European Parliament, the question as to whether or not it would be a good idea to adopt the RTBF in Canada inevitably emerged in privacy circles and sparked a heated and ongoing debate. In January 2016, the Office of the Privacy Commissioner (OPC) of Canada launched a public consultation on reputational privacy, and 28 proposals from leading academics, industry leaders, privacy lawyers, and the general public were submitted. Over half of these proposals dealt with the RTBF and most argued against it.[15] Commentators were mainly concerned that the RTBF would be an odd fit in the Canadian legal landscape. Granting individuals the right to request deletion of personal information and de-indexation of online content would impose unreasonable limits on freedom of expression[16] and may lead to unjustifiable censure.[17] The implementation of the RTBF in Canada would also prove to be difficult; search engines would now be responsible for deciding what we get to see or say,[18] a power normally held by courts.

---

14 See Google Spain SL and Google Inc v Agencia Espanola de Proteccion de Datas (AEPD) and Mario Costeja González, C-131/12, [2014] ECR I-317.
15 See OPC, "Summary of Reputation Submissions" (20 December 2017), online: *Office of the Privacy Commissioner of Canada*, https://www.priv.gc.ca/en/about-the-opc/what-we-do/consultations/consultation-on-online-reputation/submissions-received-for-the-consultation-on-online-reputation/or/or_intro/.
16 See Eloïse Gratton & Jules Polonetsky, "Privacy above all other Fundamental Rights? Challenges with the Implementation of a Right to Be Forgotten in Canada" (August 2016), online: *Office of the Privacy Commissioner of Canada*, https://www.priv.gc.ca/en/about-the-opc/what-we-do/consultations/consultation-on-online-reputation/submissions-received-for-the-consultation-on-online-reputation/or/sub_or_03/. See also Eloïse Gratton & Jules Polonetsky , "Droit à l'oubli: Canadian Perspective on the Global 'Right to Be Forgotten' Debate" (2016) 15:2 Colo Tech LJ 337.
17 See The Globe and Mail, "Submission to the OPC's Consultation on Online Reputation"(August2016),online:*OfficeofthePrivacyCommissionerofCanada*,https://www.priv.gc.ca/en/about-the-opc/what-we-do/consultations/consultation-on-online-reputation/submissions-received-for-the-consultation-on-online-reputation/or/sub_or_22/.
18 See Google Canada, "Can the Right to Be Forgotten Find Application in the Canadian Context and, If So, How?" (August 2016), online: *Office of the Privacy Commissioner of Canada*, https://www.priv.gc.ca/en/about-the-opc/what-we-do/consultations/consultation-on-online-reputation/submissions-received-for-the-consultation-on-online-reputation/or/sub_or_19/.

To further complicate the matter, it is not clear if Canadian federal and provincial privacy laws are even applicable to such entities.[19]

If most of the submissions argued against the RTBF, many also defended the idea that it should and can find its way into Canadian law. As a matter of fact, many of the submissions claimed that the core components of the RTBF can already be found in the Personal Information Protection and Electronic Document Act (PIPEDA).[20] Although some statutory guidance would still be needed,[21] principles relating to deletion of personal information, consent withdrawal, and accuracy of information may provide solid grounds on which a Canadian RTBF could stand.

This interpretation seems to have had some influence on the OPC's own work. In January 2018, the OPC published a draft position on reputational privacy where it claims that two key mechanisms of the RTBF, namely de-indexing and source takedown, are already embedded into PIPEDA.[22] Since then, the OPC has also launched a reference case asking the Federal Court to clarify if search engines are subject to PIPEDA when they index web pages and present search results that are linked to a person's name.[23]

The disruptive impact of the RTBF in privacy circles may explain why it is seen as revolutionary.[24] The RTBF introduces new and transformative ways of thinking about privacy. The right for people

---

19 See David T.S. Fraser, "You'd Better Forget the Right to Be Forgotten in Canada" (August 2016), online: *Office of the Privacy Commissioner of Canada*, https://www.priv.gc.ca/en/about-the-opc/what-we-do/consultations/consultation-on-online-reputation/submissions-received-for-the-consultation-on-online-reputation/or/sub_or_07/.

20 See Andrea Slane, "Regulating Business Models that Capitalize on User Posted Personal Information of Others: How Can Canada's Privacy Regime Protect Victims of Online Shaming Businesses?" (August 2016), online: Office of the Privacy Commissioner of Canada https://www.priv.gc.ca/en/about-the-opc/what-we-do/consultations/consultation-on-online-reputation/submissions-received-for-the-consultation-on-online-reputation/or/sub_or_01/.

21 See Christopher Berzins, "Can the Right to Be Forgotten Find Application in the Canadian Context?" (August 2016), online: https://www.priv.gc.ca/en/about-the-opc/what-we-do/consultations/consultation-on-online-reputation/submissions-received-for-the-consultation-on-online-reputation/or/sub_or_06/.

22 See OPC, Draft OPC Position on Online Reputation, *supra* note 3.

23 See OPC, "Announcement: Privacy Commissioner Seeks Federal Court Determination on Key Issue for Canadian Online Reputation" (10 October 2018), online: *Office of the Privacy Commissioner of Canada*, https://www.priv.gc.ca/en/opc-news/news-and announcements/2018/an_181010/.

24 See e.g. Reference re subsection 18.3(1) of the Federal Courts Act, RSC 1985, c F-7, 2019 FC 261(CanLII).

to decide what others can "remember" about them not only challenges existing privacy laws and principles but also contradicts online information sharing habits and practices. Yet, it also seems like the RTBF is an old idea dressed in fresh new clothes. As one author puts it, the RTBF is maybe less of a novelty than "a return to what used to be," for it "sets the stage for aligning new communications media with more traditional lifespan of information and a restoration of the eventual drawing of a curtain of obscurity over information as its timeliness fades."[25] By stressing the value of forgetfulness as a default position, advocates of the RTBF are indeed pushing less for something entirely novel than for the restoration of a time where it was possible and normal to forget. This aspiration is, I think, quite romantic.

As an artistic, political, and philosophical movement, Romanticism emerged in the early stages of the 19th century as a reaction to the Enlightenment and the scientific rationalization of nature it championed. Nature was not to be considered merely as an object of scientific inquiry, but as a source of inspiration for the development of a "new moral aesthetic"[26] that advocates a return to "natural simplicity, the ordinary, everyday rustic life."[27] For Romantics, a way of life grounded in nature enables a more genuine and spontaneous experience of life than what the cold and calculated industrial culture allows for. As such, romantic thinkers tend to express a deep attachment to the intrinsic capacities and sensibilities of human beings. They reject any idea that one could establish a clear distinction between humanity and nature, whether it be through culture, reason, or human exceptionalism. In an age that interpreted the affirmation of human knowledge and power over nature as a sign of progress, Romantics were seen as radicals, eccentrics guided by emotions who developed a particular taste for mysticism, deviance, and alternate states of mind. But Romanticism was not only radical, it was also revolutionary. It depicted the Enlightenment as an undesirable take on life and human

---

25  See Jennifer Barrigar, "Submission: Office of the Privacy Commissioner of Canada Consultation – Online Reputation" (August 2016), online: *Office of the Privacy Commissioner of Canada*, https://www.priv.gc.ca/en/about-the-opc/what-we-do/consultations/consultation-on-online-reputation/submissions-received-for-the-consultation-on-online-reputation/or/sub_or_08/.

26  See Inger S. B. Brodey, "On Pre-Romanticism or Sensibility: Defining Ambivalences" in Michael Ferber, ed, A Companion to European Romanticism (New Jersey: Wiley-Blackwell, 2005) at 19.

27  Ibid.

experience; it denounced its pitfalls and excesses; and it offered an alternative way of life that would operate a return to how things were before the Industrial Revolution. Romantics were revolutionary in the sense that they saw the past as a vector of freedom, and our natural inclinations as tools for emancipation.

One could wonder why I deem it interesting to bring up Romanticism in a text on the RTBF. I concede that it may be a bit of a stretch, but if we are to think of the emergence of this new right as a revolution in the privacy field, I think that it is useful to see that this revolution is quite romantic. Romantic in its ambition, above all, because the proponents of the RTBF seem to express a strong desire to get back to simpler times where we, as individuals and collectivities, could forget and therefore live without having all our actions, beliefs, and decisions permanently recorded and readily accessible to all. The era of total recall and perfect memory seems to have brought new vulnerabilities and concerns. By threatening our capacity to live in a present that is not heavily determined by the echoes of our old selves, technologies may limit our capacity to evolve, to change, and to reinvent ourselves. In such a context, it may seem like the room left for second chances and forgiveness is slowly disappearing. As Antoinette Rouveroy puts it, it is our natural and biological inclination to forget that grounds human autonomy and our capacity to self-govern. Moreover, second chances and pardons play an important role in law:

> Nous voulons soutenir que l'une des conditions nécessaires à l'épanouissement de l'autonomie individuelle est, pour l'individu, la possibilité d'envisager son existence non pas comme la confirmation ou la répétition de ses propres traces, mais comme la possibilité de changer de route, d'explorer des modes de vie et façons d'être nouveaux, en un mot, d'aller là où on l'attend pas. C'est bien ce "droit à une seconde chance", la possibilité de recommencer à zéro (ce que consacre déjà le droit à l'oubli lorsqu'il impose par exemple l'effacement des mentions de condamnation pénales, après un certain temps, du casier judiciaire) qu'il importe de restaurer ou de préserver, non seulement pour les personnes ayant purgé une peine criminelle, mais pour l'ensemble de la population dès lors qu'augmente la capacité de la mémoire digitale.[28]

---

28 Antoinette Rouvroy, "Réinventer l'art d'oublier et de se faire oublier dans la société de l'information" in Stéphanie Lacour, *La sécurité de l'individu numérisé. Réflexions prospectives et internationals* (Paris, L'Harmattan, 2008) at 252.

According to Rouveroy the RTBF is best understood as a right to a second chance ("ce droit à une seconde chance"), a right which can already be found in our laws. Criminal law, for example, already allows people with a criminal record to ask for pardon and allows them to start afresh. Rouveroy's main point is that, as our collective capacity to record and remember vast amount of knowledge about people, this right to a second should be extended to all. In her contribution, Jennifer Stoddart argues along similar lines, as she qualifies the RTBF as the "current reincarnation" of the RTBF in "Continental penal law" and of "great interest to just about anyone who use the Internet today."[29]

The right to decide what others know or remember about us has a direct impact on our capacity to shape our identity and reputation. Reputation has been a recurring theme in the conversation about the RTBF in Canada. In fact, concerns over reputational harm caused online have catalyzed this conversation. In 2015, the OPC identified the protection of online reputation as one of its four strategic priorities. Claiming that the Internet should be a place where individuals should be allowed to "explore their interests and develop as persons without fear that their digital trace will lead to unfair treatment," the OPC stated that our newfound capacity to never forget may have devastating long-term impacts on "our human behavior and our human relationships."[30] In order to identify possible solutions, the OPC launched a vast public consultation and a call for paper. Overall, 28 position papers were submitted to the OPC, and, as mentioned before, most of them dealt with the RTBF. These submissions were the stepping stones for the publication, in 2018, of the OPC's own Draft Position on Online Reputation, which defends the view that PIPEDA applies to search engines and grants Canadians a limited right to de-indexation.[31]

Along the same line, the Standing Committee on Access to Information, Privacy and Ethics (ETHI) released, in February 2018, a report where it explicitly addresses the RTBF in the context of online reputational privacy. Although the Committee mainly focused on the existing provisions of PIPEDA which deal with the erasure of inaccurate or outdated personal information, it also dealt with the

---

29 Jennifer Stoddart, "Lost in Translation: Transposing the Right to Be Forgotten from Different Legal Systems" (Chapter 2) at 6.

30 See OPC, "The Strategic Privacy Priorities" (2015), online: *Office of the Privacy Commissioner of Canada*, https://www.priv.gc.ca/en/about-the-opc/opc-strategic-privacy-priorities/the-strategic-privacy-priorities/#sa.

31 See OPC, "Draft OPC Position on Online Reputation", *supra* note 3.

possible recognition of a right to de-indexation in Canada and prudently recognized that such a right would be "a good way of protecting Canadians' reputation and privacy."[32] It may also be interesting to note that the recent Innovation, Science and Economic Development Canada (ISED) Proposals to modernize the Personal Information Protection and Electronic Documents Act identifies online reputation as a core concern for Canadians, but that it refuses to directly address the right to de-indexation, arguing that the debate over the application of PIPEDA to search engines is before the Federal Court.[33] The document nevertheless acknowledges the importance for minors to be able to delete or de-identify personal information held by third parties.

The idea that indexation of personal information by third parties may cause serious reputational harm has been discussed by Canadian courts on different occasions.[34] But courts and tribunals, in Canada and elsewhere, have also discussed the value of allowing people the right to delete the data private organizations have on them,[35] and stressed the dangers that the prolonged storage of personal information may pose to individual freedoms and democracy. In Carpenter, for example, the Supreme Court of the United States decided that a warrant was necessary for the State to legally access cell-site location information (CSLI) held by wireless carriers. Rejecting the notion that the third-party doctrine applies to such searches, the Supreme Court noted that, unlike "nosy neighbors," wireless carriers can today store CSLI "for years and years," in that their "memory is nearly infallible."[36] Unrestricted access to such data would grant the State "near perfect surveillance"[37] capabilities, because it would be allowed

---

32  See Standing Committee on Access to Information, Privacy and Ethics, "Towards Privacy by Design: Review of the Personal Information Protection and Electronic Documents Act" (February 2018), online: *House of Commons*, https://www.ourcommons.ca/DocumentViewer/en/42-1/ETHI/report-12/.

33  See especially IG, "Strengthening Privacy for the Digital Age" (May 2019), online: *Innovation, Science and Economic Development Canada*, https://www.ic.gc.ca/eic/site/062.nsf/eng/h_00107.html.

34  See e.g. AT v Globe24h.com, 2017 FC 114; CL c BCF Avocats d'affaires, 2016 QC-CAI 144, 2016 CarswellQue 13743.

35  See PIPEDA Report of Findings #2014-019, 2014 CanLII 99235 (PCC) (insurance provider revises retention period and practices for insurance quotes containing personal information); PIPEDA Report of Findings #2013-001, 2013 CanLII 3789 (PCC) (investigation into the personal information handling practices of WhatsApp Inc.); Halton Catholic District School Board (Re), 2015 CanLII 13372 (ON IPC); Acosta Canada Corporation (Re), 2017 CanLII 29250 (AB OIPC).

36  See Carpenter v. United States, 585 US 138 S Ct 2206, 201 L Ed 2d 507 at para 15.

37  Ibid.

to "travel back in time to retrace a person's whereabouts."[38] Prolonged retention periods of personal information, and unfettered access to the databases that store this information, would only entrench the power divergence between the State and its citizens.

But the capacity to indefinitely hold on to personal information may also transform the power structure that molds the relationships between private actors and individuals. Mayer-Schönberger, for example, argues that companies now have the means to transform the considerable amounts of information they hold about their customers into workable knowledge that can be used to exercise influence over them.[39] Contemporary literature on the manipulation of individual behaviors through data analytics, artificial intelligence, and algorithmic governance highlights the vulnerabilities to which people are exposed to due to this shifting power dynamic.[40][41] Teresa Scassa also discusses the "profound information disparity and disequilibrium" that marks our age and the growing capacity for the State and private actors to profile and surveil us.[42] Maybe one of the clearest examples of the potential dangers individual and democracies are exposed to in the age of big data is the now infamous case involving access to a massive trove of Facebook data by Cambridge Analytica for political profiling and micro-targeting purposes.[43]

Cheap storage of vast quantities of highly granular pieces of information makes retrieval and secondary uses of information possible for ends that are commendable. Keeping data alive and accessible may

---

38  Ibid at para 13.

39  Viktor Mayer-Schöenberger, *supra* note 4 at 112.

40  See e.g. Tal Z. Zarsky, "Privacy and Manipulation in the Digital Age" (2019) 30:1 Theoretical Inquiries in Law 15; Ryan Calo, "Digital Market Manipulation" (2014) 82 George Washington LR 996. See also Luke Stark, "Algorithmic Psychometrics and the Scalable Subject" (2008) 48:2 Social Studies of Science 204.

41  See Samer Hassan & Primavera de Filippi, "The Expansion of Algorithmic Governance: From Code Is Law to Law Is Code" (2017) 17 The Journal of Field Actions 88; Antoinette Rouvroy & Thomas Berns, "Gouvernementalité algorithmique et perspectives d'émancipation. Le disparate comme condition d'émancipation par la relation?" (2013) 177:1 Réseaux 163.

42  Teresa Scassa, "A Little Knowledge Is a Dangerous Thing?: Information Asymmetries and the Right to Be Forgotten" (Chapter 3) at 8.

43  See e.g. OPC, "Joint investigation of Facebook, Inc. by the Privacy Commissioner of Canada and the Information and Privacy Commissioner for British Columbia" (25 April 2019), online: Office of the Privacy Commissioner of Canada   https://www.priv.gc.ca/en/opc-actions-and-decisions/investigations/investigations-into-businesses/2019/pipeda-2019-002/.

fuel innovation and economic development,[44] drive groundbreaking research projects in precision medicine and public health,[45] and even provide better access to justice for the citizens.[46] However, the constant reactivation of the past in new and different contexts allows for new power imbalances that threaten human autonomy, individual reputations, and collective deliberative processes and structures. In this context, advocates of the RTBF believe that people should be granted the right to dim the light modern technologies shed on their past. The RTBF can thus be seen as the return of a "meta" right that was never explicitly stated by law, but that we were nevertheless granted by the practical obscurity in which our actions ineluctably and naturally fell over time.[47] This natural right, so to speak, was and remains a product of our biological configuration, a kind of original PbD.

## 3  The romantic implementation of the RTBF

The implementation of the RTBF is also, at least in Canada, somewhat romantic. The legal tools that we have at our disposal to make the RTBF operational are tributaries of a foregone era that Canadian law is, at least for the moment, desperately trying to hold on to. To be sure, there is growing support for privacy law reform, both at the legislative and doctrinal levels, but current efforts to put into action the RTBF in Canada remain grounded in a highly creative yet somehow delicate interpretation of PIPEDA, a piece of legislation that is almost 20 years old.

There are several issues associated with implementing the RTBF through PIPEDA. As they have been thoroughly discussed by Jennifer Stoddart, Andrea Slane, and Teresa Scassa in their respective contributions to this book, I will only briefly go over them. In terms of de-indexing, which represents the main challenge for the viability of the RTBF

---

44  See Sonja Zillner et al. "Big Data-Driven Innovation in Industrial Sectors", in José María Cavanillas, Edward Curry & Wolfgang Wahlster, eds, *New Horizons for a Data-Driven Economy. A Roadmap for Usage and Exploitation of Big Data in Europe* (New York City: Springer, 2016) at 169.

45  W. Nicholson Price & I. Glenn Cohen, "Privacy in the Age of Medical Big Data" (2019) 25 Nature Medicine 37.

46  See Nicolas Vermeys, "Privacy v. Transparency: How Remote Access to Court Records Forces Us to Re-examine Our Fundamental Values" in Karim Benyekhlef et al., ed, *eAccess to Justice* (Ottawa: University of Ottawa Press, 2016) at 123.

47  Antoinette Rouveroy & Thomas Berns, "Le nouveau pouvoir statistique. Ou quand le contrôle s'exerce sur un réel normé, docile et sans événement car constitué de corps 'numériques'..." (2010) 40 Multitudes 88 at 101.

within the PIPEDA framework, the key question is if PIPEDA applies to information location services such as search engines. Paragraph 4(1)(a) of PIPEDA states that the law only applies to organization that "collects, uses or discloses in the course of commercial activities." One of the arguments presented by search engines is that search results are generally free for both users and content creators. Although some results are sponsored and clearly generate revenues, most of the results associated with a query of a person's name are offered at no cost. It is therefore not clear if the tasks performed by search engine functions represent a "commercial activity" within the meaning of PIPEDA. Google's main argument is that PIPEDA does not apply to the operation of its search engine because they are provided for free.[48] As Michael Rosenstock points out, this argument may be vulnerable to a broader interpretation of Paragraph 4(1)(a) of PIPEDA. The distinction between the commercial and non-commercial elements of a search function may prove artificial because it is the free services that attract users and provide opportunity for advertisers.[49] Furthermore, the expression "in the course" of a commercial activity suggests that a specific task may not need to be inherently commercial to fall within the scope of PIPEDA.[50]

If the threshold test is met, the other main challenge of applying PIPEDA to search engines is that a string of obligations would then be imposed on them. While some of these obligations are pertinent and useful in the context of the RTBF, many of them would prove difficult to apply. In its position paper on reputational privacy, the OPC mainly relies on Principle 4.6 of Schedule 1, which states that the personal information under the control of organizations should be "as accurate, complete, and up-to-date as is necessary for the purposes for which it is to be used." According to the OPC, this principle lays the ground for a right to de-indexing. Pursuant to Principle 4.10 of Schedule 1, individuals could challenge the compliance with the accuracy principle on the basis that the information is not accurate, complete, or up-to-date.[51] If the challenge succeeds, then, pursuant to

---

48  See Reference re subsection 18.3(1), *supra* note 24 at para 8.
49  See Michael Rosenstock, "Is there a 'Right to Be Forgotten' in Canada's Personal Information Protection and Electronic Documents Act (PIPEDA)?" (2018) 14 CJLT 131 at 144.
50  Ibid.
51  PIPEDA, Principle 4.10 (holds that "An individual shall be able to address a challenge concerning compliance with the above principles to the designated individual or individuals accountable for the organization's compliance").

Principle 4.9.5 of Schedule 1,[52] the search engine has the obligation to change the search results accordingly. For the OPC, "[t]he most obvious means to make such an amendment is to de-index the offending result and remove the link."[53] The interplay between Principles 4.6, 4.10, and 4.9.5 would then, under certain circumstances, provide the basis for a right to de-indexing under the PIPEDA regime. But this creative interpretation is also quite delicate, for Schedule 1 of PIPEDA is not a menu where one can select only the principles that are deemed pertinent in a given context. If it is determined that PIPEDA applies to search engines, then all the Schedule 1 principles need to be respected. For example, Principle 4.3, which relates to consent, may prove to be problematic since search engines may have to obtain individual consent from all the people whose personal information may be found in the pages it indexes.[54] The OPC clearly recognizes that it would be absurd to ask search engines to secure such consent and suggests that Parliament fleshes out workable exceptions to consent that would allow to adequately deal with indexing practices.[55]

Another delicate issue is the role that would be unilaterally assigned to search engines: balancing privacy rights with freedom of expression and freedom of information. When faced with a de-indexing request, the responsibility to decide if the public's right to access the information is greater than the harm it may cause to the individual's privacy will fall within the hands of the organization. Search engines would then be de facto assigned an adjudicative function that they are not designed to fulfill. Moreover, as made abundantly clear in its submission to the OPC's public consultation on reputational privacy, Google does not want to play that role. As Google points out, when deciding if a link should be deleted or not, it may face a dilemma where its own interests are at play. On the one hand, the exhaustivity of its search results is diminished and it may wrongfully affect freedom of speech and freedom of information. On the other hand, it exposes itself to civil judgments or regulatory penalties.[56] As Gratton and Polonetsky argue, "Google is not an administrative tribunal exercising the quasi-judicial role of deciding the fate of the public interest in accessing certain information

---

52 PIPEDA, Principle 4.9.5 (holds that "When an individual successfully demonstrates the inaccuracy or incompleteness of personal information, the organization shall amend the information as required").
53 OPC, "Draft OPC Position on Online Reputation", *supra* note 3.
54 See Rosenstock, *supra* note 49 at 146; Slane, *supra* note 1 at 351.
55 See OPC, "Draft OPC Position on Online Reputation", *supra* note 3.
56 See Google Canada, *supra* note 18.

in Canada."[57] One of the risks associated with applying PIPEDA to search engines is therefore to turn it into a law used for governing online speech and allowing private actors to decide the fate of fundamental rights and freedom in Canada.[58]

The analysis regarding the existence of source takedown in PIPEDA is more straightforward than in the case of de-indexing. If the information to be deleted was originally shared by the person herself, then she would simply need to withdraw her consent for the information to be deleted or made anonymous pursuant to Principle 4.5.3 of Schedule 1.[59] The real difficulty lies with the information that was legally shared by third parties. The OPC acknowledges that "under PIPEDA individuals do not have an unqualified right to remove that content."[60] Nevertheless, following the same line of reasoning that leads to the conclusion that a right to de-indexing exists in PIPEDA, the OPC claims that people could challenge the accuracy of the information held by organizations, which would have the obligation to delete the information when it is demonstrably inaccurate, incomplete, or not up-to-date. This source takedown mechanism would apply when the organization was provided with the information by a third party in order, for example, to compile a profile that could be used to make a decision about the individual. This configuration would also strike for the adequate balance between privacy and freedom of speech that source takedown so clearly threatens.[61]

Despite the highly creative interpretation of PIPEDA delivered by the OPC in its Draft Position on Online Reputation, the implementation of the RTBF may prove delicate in the Canadian context. While the decision of the Federal Court in the reference case will provide valuable cues to assess the validity of the OPC's interpretation, the debate on the viability of the RTBF in Canada remains molded by the constraints imposed by PIPEDA. These constraints not only make it difficult for the RTBF to find a comfortable footing in the Canadian legal landscape but also makes it hard for the debate on the RTBF to

---

57  See also Gratton & Polonetsky, *supra* note 16 at 43.

58  See e.g. Daphne Keller, "A Right to Be Forgotten in Canada?" (May 2018), online: *Center for Internet and Society*, http://cyberlaw.stanford.edu/blog/2018/05/right-be-forgotten-canada.

59  PIPEDA, Principle 4.5.3 (holds that "Personal information that is no longer required to fulfil the identified purposes should be destroyed, erased, or made anonymous").

60  OPC, "Draft OPC Position on Online Reputation", *supra* note 3.

61  Ibid.

move beyond de-indexing and source takedown. As Canadian jurists and stakeholders work on fleshing out these two core mechanisms, an important dimension of the RTBF remains unaddressed. I pointed out in the introduction that for the noble ambitions of the RTBF to be achieved, privacy law should pay greater attention to how perfect memory is generated in the first place. To protect people from the vulnerabilities raised by this age of total recall, it might be necessary to not only focus on how to make PIPEDA workable but also think about how to move pass PIPEDA.

## 4 Moving forward: design and group power

The introduction of PbD in Canadian privacy law would contribute to achieving the RTBF's principal objectives. This argument rests on a set of two assumptions. First, the program of the RTBF is valid and important, but in order to solve the privacy issues it is concerned with, close attention must be paid to the automatic and continuous generation of information by modern IT systems. As I mentioned in the introduction, the best way to grant individuals and groups control over who remembers what about them may be to increase control over initial data release. Second, privacy should not be viewed only as an umbrella term for seclusion and secret. In my opinion, privacy has everything to do with sharing and striving to achieve common goals. Allowing individuals and groups to decide when, to whom, and for what purposes they will communicate intimate details about their lives does not only pay tribute to their autonomy and dignity, it can also make them active participants in the pursuit of collective projects. Protecting privacy and confidentiality contributes to enhancing the trust which is necessary for people to interact and share with others.

The current privacy legal framework in Canada mainly attributes to the individual the responsibility to protect his own privacy. Private organizations also have some responsibilities: they must notify users when their information is collected, used, or communicated and provide them with information on their privacy policies and practices. But once consent is secured, organizations have roughly fulfilled their main obligations. Because some of the most important aspects of our lives are experienced online, interacting with technology is not as much a choice as a necessity.[62] In such a context, securing individual consent is not a big hurdle. Moreover, people rarely read privacy policies and

---

62 See *Douez v Facebook, Inc*, 2017 SCC 33, [2017] 1 SCR 751 at para 56.

terms of use,[63] which gives tremendous power to companies to use our data as they wish. Traditional notice and consent models therefore seem more interested in looking after the interest of big data-driven companies than in protecting privacy.

Since the collection, use, and communication of personal information is deemed voluntary, one might argue that we are the ones responsible for diminishing our own privacy. After all, it is in our control to read and understand the privacy policies and the term of use to which we consent. As Bernard Harcourt rightfully claims, "we are not so much coerced, surveilled, or secured today as we are exposing or exhibiting ourselves knowingly."[64] At the same time, increased online visibility is not entirely a matter of individual choice. Many technologies are deliberately designed to nudge us into adopting certain behaviors and making particular decisions.[65] Interface design and architecture can "trick us" into sharing more information than we initially expected or wanted.[66] As the Supreme Court of Canada noted in R. c. Vu, connected devices will often automatically, and without our knowledge, generate highly specific pieces of information about our interaction with the technologies.[67] Moreover, we sometimes think we delete the information on our devices or applications, but it is not because it is no longer available on our personal profile that it is not stored somewhere in a third party's server.[68] The "data deluge" that pervasive forms of collection permit is contributing to the creation of the perfect memory the RTBF seeks to limit.[69] Designing technology that will not contribute to the surreptitious data collection frenzy is of paramount importance in the context of the RTBF.

---

63  See OPC, "2016 Survey of Canadians on Privacy" (January 2017), online: https://www. priv.gc.ca/en/opc-actions-and-decisions/research/explore-privacy-research/2016/ por_2016_12/.

64  See Bernard E. Harcourt, *Exposed. Desire and Disobedience in the Digital Age* (Cambridge: Harvard University Press, 2015) at 19.

65  What Frishmann et Selinger define as "techno-social engineering". See Brett Frishmann & Evan Selinger, *Re-Engineering Humanity* (Cambridge University Press, 2018) at 4, 67 and 120.

66  Woodrow Hartzog, *Privacy's Blueprint: The Battle to Control the Design of New Technologies* (Cambridge: Harvard University Press, 2018) at 93.

67  R v Vu, 2013 SCC 60, [2013] 3 SCR 657 at para 42.

68  Ibid at para 43.

69  Jean-François Blanchette, "The Noise in the Archive: Oblivion in the Age of Total Recall" in Serge Gutwirth, Yves Poullet, Paul De Hert & Ronald Leenes, eds, *Computers, Privacy and Data Protection: An Element of Choice* (New York: Springer, 2016) at 25.

It might be rightfully argued that personal information and sensitive data stored in third parties servers and private databases are not what the RTBF seeks to regulate or delete. As mentioned previously, the RTBF focuses on de-indexing and is mainly geared toward search engines. My point is that, although this distinction is meaningful, the reputational issues and privacy concerns raised by the debate surrounding the RTBF are not exclusive to search engine and information available online. In order to best manage the social risks stemming from the perfect memory modern technologies have built, privacy law should not solely focus on publicly available information but on all data collected and stored by private or public actors. In her contribution to this book, Andrea Slane brilliantly discusses the profiling techniques used by private actors to scrape, assemble, and share data found online about a particular person and how online profiles have become a central component or our social identity.[70] The GDPR defines profiling as:

> any form of automated processing of personal data consisting of the use of personal data to evaluate certain personal aspects relating to a natural person, in particular to analyse or predict aspects concerning that natural person's performance at work, economic situation, health, personal preferences, interests, reliability, behaviour, location or movements.[71]

Predictions and evaluations based on highly sensitive information can be used in decision-making processes which can have a significant impact on a person's life. Search engines are obviously not the only actors compiling such profiles, nor are all profiles exclusively made of information gathered online. Social networks such as Facebook, online platforms such as Netflix, and companies such as Apple also create extensive profiles from the data automatically generated by the users' interaction with their technology. Moreover, because this information is highly valuable, it is rarely shared by companies or made available online. Teresa Scassa makes a highly important point when she claims that:

> [d]e-indexing of internet content will change what ordinary individuals are able to know about other people; it will not change

---

70 See Andrea Slane, "Reconciling Privacy and Expression Rights by Regulating Profile Compilation Services" (Chapter 4).
71 GDPR, *supra* note 5, art 4(4).

what corporations or governments are able to know. This is why, apart from all of the other complexities of implementing a right to be forgotten and of balancing it with freedom of expression and other values, we need to tread very carefully. Information asymmetries are very real and very harmful. We should avoid making them worse.[72]

The RTBF will indeed limit what ordinary people can know about other people without limiting the State and private actors' profiling and surveillance efforts. Implementing the RTBF without restricting these actors data collection schemes and strategies may well end up accentuating the existing power imbalances. It therefore seems highly relevant for privacy law to limit the initial collection of these massive quantities of personal information and superimpose a PbD approach over an eventual RTBF.

How and to what extent privacy laws should govern the design of technology is a difficult question. One place to start is to identify a model on which rules and standards can be built. Privacy principles found in Schedule 1 of PIPEDA may intuitively come to mind. Designs should be focused, for example, on enhancing transparency, informing consent, or securing data. Yet, these principles may not suffice. They might be helpful to fix broader goals and general rules, but they were not elaborated to guide design practices or to mitigate their effects. Luckily, other fields of the law have developed strong and flexible regimes that could serve as models for guiding design with privacy law. Woodrow Hartzog convincingly argues that product safety and consumer protection are credible candidates. Product safety is interested in preventing the sale of dangerous products and incentivizes transparent communication of the risks associated with its use. As such, product safety focuses on effective warnings, disclaimers, and instructions that can set people's expectations. One key point of product safety is that companies may be liable for the harm caused by their products even if it results from a misuse of the product.[73] This is important, because it means that companies have to be honest and transparent with their consumers. When a person buys and uses a product, the company who sells it to her cannot simply walk away.

According to Hartzog, effective warnings are a better option than the ineffective notice and consent model. While a warning is given to a

---

72  Scassa, *supra* note 42.
73  Hartzog, *supra* note 66 at 126.

person to inform of possible risks associated with a behavior, consent is taken from a person as a form authorization to engage in risky behavior.[74] The former keeps the company liable and responsible, while the latter seems to put the ultimate responsibility in the hands of the user. In other words, with the notice and consent model, "we bear the burden of responsibility for them."[75] As mentioned before, current notice and consent model are highly problematic. If people do not read the terms of use or the privacy policies of the devices or applications they use – often because they are designed not to be read – then it is difficult to conclude that people exercise meaningful control over the personal information they share with different companies. Clear and efficient communication in the form of warnings about the type of data that will be collected and the risk associated with these uses could increase meaningful control over personal information.[76]

Consumer protection law also provides interesting solutions for enhancing privacy protection through the design of technology. One of the fundamental missions of consumer protection law is to prevent and punish the exploitation of vulnerabilities stemming from our use of a product. As mentioned in part 1, the use of technology in the age of perfect memory creates power imbalances and new opportunities for the manipulation of opinion and behaviors. The exploitation of human vulnerabilities and cognitive bias through design may come in different forms. Designs can be deceptive, in that they send false signals or omit to send valuable ones to users. Privacy policies that omit or "burry" certain data collection practices, for example, would be considered as deceptive. Here, warnings can play an important role. Instead of simply informing in an approximative way people about how their data will be collected, used, or disclosed, companies should have to clearly warn users about the implication of sharing their data.[77] Again, such practice would fix people's expectations and allow information sharing behaviors based on concrete information. Moreover, increasing openness and accountability would foster trust and, when the context is appropriate, encourage sharing.

74  Ibid at 129–130.
75  See Ari Ezra Waldman, *Privacy as Trust. Information Privacy for an Information Age* (New York: Cambridge University Press, 2018) at 32.
76  See Déziel, *supra* note 13 at 845 (one problem facing this approach, especially in regard to AI techniques, is the difficulty to identify all the possible uses to which the data could be put before the data are collected).
77  Hartzog, *supra* note 66 at 140.

Designs can also be abusive.[78] A design will be abusive when it plays on cognitive limits in order to trick us into doing things. The more we share with a company, the more it knows about us. And the more it knows about us, the easier it becomes to identify our soft spots and predict our behavior. With personalization approaches and data-linkage techniques that are increasingly sophisticated, it becomes easier for companies to extract and generate new knowledge, often at our great surprise.[79] Because consumer protection laws target companies that use deceptive and abusive designs, it can play an important role in making sure that designs are not used to unreasonably exploit privacy vulnerabilities. As Hartzog argues, product safety and consumer protection law are viable models on which a PbD approach could be built. As a result, we should aim for privacy laws that:

> Discourage design that tricks us, lies to us, exploit us, or dangerously weakens or destroys practical hiding places for our personal information. Such technologies betray our trust and threaten the obscurity we rely upon to make autonomous choices.[80]

Designs have an effect on the automatic and spontaneous generation of information that feeds our individual and collective perfect memories. They facilitate blind sharing and allow companies to collect and use massive quantities of information about us. The notice and consent model, which is at the heart of PIPEDA, does not prevent this endemic data stockpiling. If our personal information is collected without clear warnings, it may then be difficult for us to exercise our RTBF. But better design could also allow for more meaningful control over our personal information, which, in turn, could contribute to honest and voluntary data-sharing practices that could empower individuals and collectivities. This is in part why PbD framework has to be considered in the debate on the RTBF.

## 5 Conclusion

To conclude, I will make two quick points on why the debate on the RTBF is important for privacy law. First, I think that the specific and highly technical debate on the RTBF in Canada is illuminating for

---

78  Ibid at 142.
79  See Sheri B. Pan., "Get to Know Me" (2016) 30:1 Harv JL & Tech 249 at 254.
80  Hartzog, *supra* note 66 at 126.

privacy law in general. The issues raised by advocates and critics of the RTBF are touching on ideas and notions that are broader than de-indexing and source takedown. They point to systemic problems, such as power imbalances, mistrust, freedom of speech, and the inadequacies of notice and consent. These concerns have to be addressed in a comprehensive way and through drastic reform. In that sense, it might be time to let go of the past and turn the RTBF into something more than a romantic revolution. Second, I think that privacy law cannot deal with these issues on its own. It might need help from outside. Criminal law, for example, can already be of tremendous help in dealing with cases of the non-consensual publication of intimate images. As discussed in the last section, seeking the help of product safety and consumer protection law might be highly beneficial from a privacy standpoint. In other words, privacy law in Canada should start looking not only ahead but also to its side.

# 6    The right to be forgotten in peace processes

*Ignacio N. Cofone and*
*Catalina Turriago Betancourt*

## 1 Introduction

The right to be forgotten (RTBF) has been a contested topic of discussion for decades. A large body of literature has focused on its advantages, dangers, and applications in both deleting and delisting information from search results about embarrassing or humiliating events, negative financial information, and criminal records.[1] But there is another potentially useful and highly consequential application that remains unexplored: the RTBF has the potential to facilitate peace processes. Peace processes seek to put an end to internal, often militarized, conflicts within States through the implementation of different political arrangements that reintegrate former combatants into society.[2] In this context, the RTBF could, within certain parameters we discuss, favor reconciliation and peace.

This essay is, to our knowledge, the first to explore the possible application of the RTBF in peace processes. As such, we aim not to provide a definitive normative suggestion but to canvass the reasons in favor and against such application and when these reasons may lead to its fruitful implementation. To do so, we examine how the RTBF would operate in these contexts and how it may conflict with other rights, namely free speech, access to information, and victims' rights.

While a common goal of peace processes is reconciliation, not all processes pursue it in the same way,[3] as both desirable and plausible measures depend on the social and institutional context of the

---

1 See Chapters 1–5.
2 Jonathan Tonge, *Comparative Peace Processes* (Cambridge, UK: Polity Press, 2014) at 7.
3 Jeremy Sarkin & Erin Daly, "Too Many Questions, Too Few Answers: Reconciliation in Transitional Societies" (2004) Colum HRLR at 725.

transitioning jurisdiction. Thus, any application of the RTBF in peace processes will be context-sensitive: different post-conflict societies will reach different conclusions about how to balance the interests involved.

We focus on the application of the RTBF to former members of armed forces as a tool that countries could adopt within peace processes to facilitate reconciliation among former armed forces members, victims, and citizens. We trace three conditions for its implementation. First, the application of the RTBF should be limited to those individuals who were lawfully granted amnesty – and not those who committed crimes excluded from amnesty.[4] Second, the RTBF should typically consist of not deleting information, but delisting references to amnestied individuals on search results that connect them to the acts they received a lawful amnesty for.[5] Third, such delisting should not interfere with information of heightened public interest. These are not sufficient conditions to reap the benefits of the RTBF, but necessary ones. An application within these boundaries, depending on the social and institutional context, may facilitate reintegration without affecting historical records and victims' rights.

## 2 Achieving peace

### 2.1 What is a peace process?

In situations following internal conflict, countries face pivotal social and political changes that can involve either a transition from an authoritarian regime to a democracy or from conflict to peace.[6] The transition from conflict to peace (with or without a regime change), which we will call peace process, is the transitional process we focus on.

The main goal of peace processes is to achieve reconciliation among the affected parties so that they can coexist peacefully.[7] The role and

---

4 In addition, within granted amnesties, there may be good reasons to exclude those who committed crimes against humanity, genocide, or war crimes, as we explore below.
5 See Ignacio N. Cofone, "Google v. Spain: A Right to Be Forgotten?" (2015) 15 Chicago-Kent J Intl & Comp L 1 for an explanation on the different types of right to be forgotten.
6 Gloria Zambrano Ramón, "Memoria y Reparación: el Camino de la Justicia Transicional para las Víctimas", in Jairo Becerra, ed, *Fundamentación y aplicabilidad de la justicia transicional en Colombia* (Bogotá: Universidad Católica de Colombia, 2016) at 122.
7 Sarkin & Daly, *supra* note 3 at 665.

scope of such reconciliation will be drastically affected by the social and institutional context. While most agree that there is no one size fits all for reconciliation processes, which differ among societies,[8] many add that their success universally depends on the respect of victims' rights.[9] The main goal of these processes is reconciliation,[10] but reconciliation should not be used as an excuse to violate victims' rights.[11]

Central to peace processes, from a transitional justice perspective, are the victims.[12] According to this body of literature, peace processes' essential elements in pursuing its aims of ending the war are victims' reparation, and the rights to the truth, historical memory, and justice.[13] The right to truth refers to victims' right to know what happened during the conflict.[14] The right to historical memory aims to uncover the origins of the conflict and events that lead to such wrongs,[15] sometimes framed as victims' rights and sometimes as a right of society at large.[16] The right to justice consists on the investigation and prosecution of those who were responsible for such wrongs.[17]

Every transition from armed conflict to peace, regardless of its particularities, faces a major challenge: if offenders believe they will not reintegrate successfully, they are unlikely to support the peace agreement. As Tonge points out, peace processes entail "painful compromises and often further hurt for families of victims of the conflicts, as perpetrators may re-enter society."[18] The future discrimination of

---

8   Ibid at 725.
9   Zambrano, *supra* note 6 at 122.
10  Sarkin & Daly, *supra* note 3 at 665.
11  Zambrano, *supra* note 6 at 122.
12  Eric Sottas, "Transitional Justice and Sanctions" (2008) 90 Intl Rev Red Cross at 337.
13  Zambrano, *supra* note 6 at 121.
14  Sam Szoke-Burke, "Searching for the Right to Truth: The Impact of International Human Rights Law on National Transitional Justice Policies" (2015) 33:2 BJIL at 532–533; Organization of American States, Inter-American Commission on Human Rights, *Derecho a la Verdad en América* (2014) at 33–34.
15  See e.g. Laura Zazueta Carrillo, "The Right to the Truth in the Context of Transitional Justice as an Obligation of the Mexican State in the Face of Impunity" (2014) 9:2 VIeI.
16  See e.g. Anna Bryson, "Victims, Violence, and Voice: Transitional Justice, Oral History, and Dealing with the Past" (2016) 39:2 Hastings Intl & Comp L Rev 299; Kirsten Campbell, "The Laws of Memory: The ICTY, the Archive, and Transitional Justice" (2013) 22:2 Soc & Leg Stud 247; Martha Minow, *Between Vengeance and Forgiveness* (United States of America: Beacon Press, 1998).
17  See e.g. Szoke-Burke, *supra* note 14 at 546–547, and Anne-Marie La Rosa & Xavier Philippe, "Transitional Justice" in Vincent Chetail, ed, *Post-conflict Peacebuilding: A Lexicon* (Oxford: Oxford University Press, 2009).
18  Tonge, *supra* note 2 at 11.

former offenders and other individuals linked to the conflict as those individuals reintegrate into society can threaten the viability of the peace process.

To evidence this problem, we refer to the conflicts of Rwanda, Northern Ireland, and Colombia. While we cannot fully cover the history, causes, and consequences of these conflicts, we highlight that, despite their differences, these conflicts and their peace processes illustrate the problem of rejection from civil society of offenders or individuals connected to the conflict as they try to reincorporate into civilian life.

## 2.2 Why the RTBF in peace processes?

The 1994 Rwandan genocide had roots in colonial era when "an elite group of Tutsi exploited Hutu as second-class citizens."[19] During the 1950s, Hutus freed themselves from Tutsi domination in a movement that led to deaths, destruction, and "flight of tens of thousands of Tutsis to neighboring countries."[20] Later on, Tutsi rebel refugees seeking to return to power launched failed attacks that, in turn, triggered oppression of Tutsis, massive killings, and the fleeing of about half of the Tutsi population from Rwanda.[21] Violence between Hutus and Tutsis continued sporadically for the next 30 years.[22] People's fear and hatred against Tutsis intensified when the Arusha Accords were signed, which were considered too favorable to Tutsis,[23] and Hutus feared that Tutsi rebels would eventually conquer and dominate Rwanda.[24] Distrust against Tutsis increased when Tutsi rebels assassinated Burundi's first Hutu president.[25] The Tutsi genocide was triggered when Rwandan President Habyarimana was assassinated.[26] Although it was unclear who committed the attack, Hutu groups blamed the Tutsis and government radio as well as extremist media "urged Hutu to take vengeance against Tutsi for their alleged murder of the president."[27]

---

19 Alan J. Kuperman, *The Limits of Humanitarian Intervention: Genocide in Rwanda* (Washington, DC: Brookings Institution Press, 2001) at 6.
20 Ibid at 7.
21 Ibid.
22 Alison Desforges, *Leave None to tell the Story* (Human Rights Watch, 1999) at 9. For example, President Habyarimana and others exaggerated the Tutsi rebels' threat widening divisions between Hutus and Tutsis.
23 Ibid.
24 Kuperman, *supra* note 19 at 12.
25 Ibid at 11–12.
26 Ibid.
27 Kuperman, *supra* note 19 at 15.

The genocide produced over 800,000 victims, with a killing rate twice as fast as the Nazi Holocaust.[28] Approximately three-quarters of the Rwandan Tutsi population was murdered.[29]

After the genocide, the Rwandan community was left torn. It had become a common assumption among Rwandans and outsiders that "all Hutu killed Tutsi, or at least actively participated in the genocide in some way."[30] The almost one million deaths, the feeling that all Hutus were collectively responsible for them, and the perception of an inadequate delivery of justice produced resentment and hate toward Hutu. The Rwandan Government condemned to death and executed individuals who allegedly participated in the genocide in public stadiums, in front of spectators who celebrated the event.[31] These executions were criticized because, besides their violence, many condemned individuals did not have counsel during the trial, increasing the possibility of wrongful convictions.[32] At the same time, it was a widespread belief among the population that there was "inadequate delivery of justice."[33] Desire for revenge took over Rwanda. Accused individuals lacked legal defense because most Rwandan lawyers refused to represent defendants accused of acts related to the genocide.[34] As Martha Minow points out, "rather than ending cycles of revenge, the trials themselves were revenge."[35] Feelings of resentment, sadness, loss of trust, fear, shame, and humiliation remained in the victims after the genocide.[36] Resentment and distrust among the community continue to hinder effective reconciliation.[37]

Another well-known conflict that illustrates the problem of reintegration took place in Northern Ireland.[38] It was labeled as one of the "most intractable and violent nationalist conflicts in

28  Astri Suhrke & Howard Adelman, *The Path of a Genocide: The Rwanda Crisis from Uganda to Zaire* (New York: Routledge, 1999) at xviii.
29  Desforges, *supra* note 22 at 18.
30  Ibid at 567.
31  Ibid at 583.
32  Ibid.
33  Ibid at 568.
34  Minow, *supra* note 16 at 124.
35  Ibid.
36  Thomas Brudholm & Valerie Rosoux, "The Unforgiving: Reflections on the Resistance to Forgiveness after Atrocity" in Alexander Keller Hirsch, ed, *Theorizing Post-Conflict Reconciliation: Agonism, Restitution and Repair* (Milton Park, Abingdon, Oxon Routledge, 2012) at 124–125.
37  Chris McGreal, "Rwanda Genocide 20 Years On: 'We Live with those Who Killed Our Families. We Are Told They're Sorry, but Are They?" *The Guardian* (12 May 2013).
38  Amaia Alvarez Berastegi, "Transitional Justice in Settled Democracies: Northern Ireland and the Basque Country in Comparative Perspective" (2017) 10:3 Crit Stud on Terrorism at 543.

Western Europe."[39] The causes of the conflict were complex and contested,[40] involving religious (Catholic and Protestant)[41] and territorial (Irish-British international border) issues.[42] The conflict ended in 1998 having produced over 3,600 victims.[43]

Although the peace process in Northern Ireland was considered successful,[44] many have criticized the agreement that concluded it. It was argued that the peace process "did not resolve fully the issues under dispute, as each side continues to interpret the conflict through its own lens (...) and remains distrustful of its former enemies."[45] Scholars have suggested that Northern Ireland failed to expose the truth during the conflict, increasing fear and lack of trust.[46] Due to the biased interpretation of the conflict and mistrust, individuals who were connected or perceived to be connected to the Troubles could be rejected by civilians.

Another conflict that illustrates this dynamic is Colombia's current peace process. One of the main rebel groups in Colombia's internal armed conflict is the *Fuerzas Armadas Revolucionarias de Colombia* (FARC), which has contributed to Colombia's violence and armed conflict for over 50 years. The FARC's origins can be traced back to *La Violencia* period that commenced in 1948,[47] but since 1970, the FARCs have also been involved in drug trafficking,[48] assassinations, kidnapping, and extortions.[49] By 2002, Colombia had the highest rate of kidnapping and murders worldwide.[50]

---

39  Michael Keating, "Northern Ireland and the Basque Country" in John McGarry, *Northern Ireland and the Divided World: Post-Agreement Northern Ireland in Comparative* (Oxford: Oxford Scholarship Online, 2003) at 1.

40  William Hazleton, "Look at Northern Ireland" in Timothy J. White ed., *Lessons from the Northern Island Peace Processes* (Wisconsin: University of Wisconsin Press, 2013) at 35.

41  Timothy J White, et al., "Extending Peace to the Grassroots: The Need for Reconciliation in Northern Ireland after the Agreement" in Timothy J White ed, *Lessons from the Northern Island Peace Processes* (Wisconsin: University of Wisconsin Press, 2013) at 228.

42  Ibid at 229.

43  Alvarez, *supra* note 38 at 545.

44  Hazleton, *supra* note 40 at 36.

45  White, et al., *supra* note 41 at 227.

46  Ibid at 253–254.

47  Norman Offstein, "A Historical Review and Analysis of Colombian Guerrilla Movements: FARC, ELN and EPL" (2003) 52 Desarrollo y Sociedad at 101.

48  Ibid at 108.

49  Rene Provost, "FARC Justice: Rebel Rule of Law" (2018) 8 UC Irvine L Rev at 234.

50  Miguel Silva, "El camino hacia la prosperidad, el milagro colombiano", Report, (2015) Atlantic Council. Adrienne Arsht Latin American Center at 3.

Several attempts by the Colombian Government to sign peace agreements with the FARC have failed.[51] However, between 2002 and 2010, the FARC started to weaken and retract.[52] In this context, in 2012 the government started a new negotiation attempt.[53] After multiple rounds of negotiations, in 2016 the Government and the FARC agreed to a peace agreement on the termination of the armed conflict which was subject to a plebiscite in 2016.[54] Colombian citizens were asked whether they supported the agreement.[55] 49.78% voted in favor and 50.21% against.[56] The victory of "the NO" resulted in multiple revisions of the final agreement.[57] On November 2016, the government and the FARC signed a peace agreement that, aiming to attain reconciliation,[58] included several tools to facilitate the reincorporation of former FARC members.[59] However, due to the length and nature of the conflict, the extent to which former FARC members can effectively reincorporate remains unclear.

### 2.3  The credible commitment problem

The conflicts in Rwanda, Northern Ireland, and Colombia illustrate that, despite the differences regarding their causes and the mechanisms to end them, any internal war affects civilians in the long run. When a society lives through a conflict of these characteristics, it is likely that former members of the group and non-members who were connected to the conflict will be stigmatized and, understandably, a large fraction of society will fear or distrust them. Feelings in reaction to these wrongs include long-lasting "deep sadness, fear and loss of trust."[60] This situation is problematic as distrust and fear hinder

---

51  Offstein, *supra* note 47 at 109.
52  Alvaro Villarraga Sarmiento, "Los acuerdos de paz Estado-Guerrillas en Colombia, 1982–2016" (2016) 14:28 Derecho y Realidad at 114.
53  Ibid at 114.
54  See generally Colombian Constitution, art. 103, and Law 134, 1994 (art. 7).
55  Colombia, *Decree 1391*, 2016, art 1.
56  Colombia's National Civil Registry, Results of the Plebiscite held on October 2, 2016 (October 2016).
57  Villarraga, *supra* note 52 at 114.
58  Colombia, National Authority, Final Agreement to End the Armed Conflict and Build a Stable and Lasting Peace (2016) at 8. See also Fatou Bensouda, Statement of ICC Prosecutor on the conclusion of the peace negotiations between the Government of Colombia and the Revolutionary Armed Forces of Colombia, https://www.icc-cpi.int/Pages/item.aspx?name=160901-otp-stat-colombia.
59  E.g. Colombia, *Law 1820*, 2016.
60  Brudholm & Rosoux, *supra* note 36 at 122.

reincorporation of offenders into civilian life, and, absent an effective reincorporation and reconciliation process, neither can a lasting peace be achieved, nor can guarantees of non-recurrence be given.

Political science literature describes this situation as a standard credible commitment problem. When a majority group offers a peace process, the minority group can either reject the peace or agree to stop fighting and accede to a political process that implements certain benefits. The credible commitment problem refers to the inability of majority groups in domestic conflicts to credibly show minority groups that they will be treated favorably if they agree to the peace process in order to make the peace agreement persuasive.

Minority groups fear that if they agree to disarm and the majority group reneges on their offer, they can choose to fight again but will have lower chances of winning.[61] This means that, when offered an agreement, such minority groups are more likely to choose violence over disarming because they fear that the majority group will renege on their commitment after bargaining.[62] These conditions put groups in vulnerable positions that encourage them to renege the peace settlement.[63] Since the credible commitment problem increases the likelihood of failure of peace settlement, putting in place processes and measures to overcome it is necessary for post-conflict peace.[64]

Amnesties are sometimes deployed to overcome this credible commitment problem. Defined as "acts of forgiveness that a sovereign State grants to individuals who have committed criminal acts,"[65] amnesties forego criminal liability of possible offenders who do not go through a criminal trial that determines their culpability.[66] Relatively

---

61 See Edward Thomas Flores & Irfan Nooruddin, "Credible Commitment in Post Conflict Recovery" in Christopher J. Coyne & Rachel L. Mathers, eds, *The Handbook on the Political Economy of War* (Northampton, MA: Edward Edgar Publishing, 2011) at 474; Fearon, James D., "Commitment Problems and the Spread of Ethnic Conflict" in David Lake & Donald Rothchild, eds, *The International Spread of Ethnic Conflict* (Princeton, NJ: Princeton University Press, 1998) at 107–126.

62 Ibid.

63 Hirotaka Ohmura, "Termination and Recurrence of Civil War: Which Outcomes Lead to Durable Peace after Civil War?" (2011) 12:3 Japanese J P Sci at 375; Barbara F. Walter, "The Critical Barrier to Civil War Settlement" (1997) 51:3 Intl Org at 339.

64 See Thomas & Nooruddin, *supra* note 61 at 474.

65 Evode Kayitana, "Transitional Justice: Reconciling Domestic Amnesty with the Universal Jurisdiction of Foreign States" (2017) 8 Nnamdi Azikiwe U J Intl L & Juris at 1.

66 Ibid at 1.

common in peace processes with the aim of attaining reconciliation,[67] they are used to incentivize actors to end hostilities,[68] and to maintain the existence of democratic regimes after political transitions.[69] Some scholars criticize amnesties on the grounds that they sacrifice goals of justice,[70] while others argue that they can contribute to the fulfillment of transitional goals.[71] One of the major dilemmas in transitions is whether to punish or to grant amnesty.[72]

Not all amnesties are lawful, however. Of particular legal controversy is whether amnesties can be applied at all to war crimes and crimes involving gross human rights violations, such as crimes against humanity and genocide. As a result, a number of amnesty laws and arrangements may be granted but later on deemed unlawful.[73] Similarly, some amnesties are procedurally richer than others in ensuring justice through accountability as well as maintaining a historical record through legal or public proceedings. When we explore, below, the application of the RTBF to some amnesties, we do so for amnesties that are recognized to be legitimate by the international community.

Della Morte refers to amnesties as a "form of legal oblivion."[74] Given their meaning and effects, the very existence of amnesties shows that the concepts of forgetting and forgiving are not alien to the processes in which they are applied. But amnesties have no way of addressing informal societal responses. In particular, vivid memories about past atrocities committed by a certain group can encourage individuals to hurt other members of the community who belong to such group, as occurred in Rwanda.[75] Since the RTBF has been considered as "a right to be forgiven for past indecencies or wrongs,"[76] parallels exist

---

67  Sarkin & Daly, *supra* note 3 at 678; Gabriele Della Morte, "International Law between the Duty of Memory and the Right to Oblivion" (2014) 14 Special Issue: Armenian Genocide Reparations Intl Crim L Re at 431–432.

68  Kayitana, *supra* note 65 at 4.

69  Ibid at 5.

70  Joe Edet & B. E. Kooffreh, "Transitional Justice in Post Conflict Societies: Underscoring the Debates on Amnesty versus Victims' Rights" (2018) 73 J L Pol'y & Globalization at 143–144.

71  Ruti Teitel, *Transitional Justice* (New York: Oxford University Press, 2000) at 59.

72  Ibid at 27.

73  Lisa J. LaPlante, "Outlawing Amnesty: The Return of Criminal Justice in Transitional Justice Schemes" (2009) 49:4 Va J Intl L 915.

74  Della Morte, *supra* note 67 at 431.

75  Minow, *supra* note 16 at 11.

76  Chelsea E. Carbone, "To Be or Not to Be Forgotten: Balancing the Right to Know with the Right to Privacy in the Digital Age" (2015) 22 Va J Soc Pol & L at 553.

among them. However, there is no precedent in the world regarding the application of the RTBF to actors involved in them.

## 3 The RTBF as a tool to reduce credible commitment problems and facilitate reconciliation

### 3.1 Technology amplifies reputational harms under credible commitment problems

The challenge of social reinsertion in a context of credible commitment problems is amplified by technology. In the past, if negative information about individuals, including their connection with an armed conflict, was publicly circulated, its accessibility was physically and temporarily restricted.[77] This dissemination was limited by geographical restrictions and its availability was limited by its physical nature. Such information would have been contained in print such as in newspapers, books, physical criminal reports, or other archives that, unless an individual knew where to look and what information she or he was seeking, it would have been difficult to come across.[78] Information spread slowly and was received by fewer – usually those with the most serious interest in it.[79] Moreover, some information could disappear, get lost, or be destroyed.

That is how information about peace processes was stored and shared until the internal conflicts of Northern Ireland and Colombia. Until three decades ago, any information connecting former members of the armed forces to the conflict would have been limitedly available, restrictively accessible, and even partially destroyed. This reduced the risk of reputational harms to such individuals during their reincorporation process.

Ireland's and Colombia's peace processes, and all peace processes that will take place as from now, take place in the digital era, in which the "internet never forgets."[80] Transitioning from an armed conflict

---

77 Christopher Berzins, "Publicity and Privacy in Administrative Adjudication: A Right to be Forgotten" (2011) 39 Adv Q at 4.

78 Ibid at 5.

79 Viktor, Mayer-Schönberger, *Delete: The Virtue of Forgetting in the Digital Age* (Princeton, NJ: Princeton University Press, 2011), at 86–87.

80 Karl E Gustafson et al., "The Internet Never Forgets: Google Inc.'s 'right to be forgotten' EU Ruling and Its Implications in Canada", *McMillan LLP* (August 2014), online: https://mcmillan.ca/mobile/The-Internet-Never-Forgets-Google-Incs-right-to-be-forgotten-EU-ruling-and-its-implications-in-Canada.

to peace today involves greater challenges than in the past because, currently, information about such violent past and its actors is preserved in a system of perfect memory,[81] reducing the likelihood of effective reincorporation. As Deziel points out, the digital era might determine our present based on our past, jeopardizing our ability to change and reducing second chances.[82]

The internet's ubiquitous reach and ease of access also mean that information that was previously restricted is now pervasive.[83] The internet facilitates information's quick dissemination and ease of access,[84] and allows old information to outlive the context in which it was published.[85] In addition, search engines usually present the most relevant information at the top of the list of results.[86] Given that armed conflicts are extraordinary events, it is likely that any search about an individual involved will show results connecting him or her with the conflict high on the list, increasing the visibility of this information.

Reincorporation is complex because of the serious harms society and victims suffered.[87] For example, Colombia's conflict caused "more than eight million victims all over the country, around 220,000 deaths (most of them civilians), at least 25,000 kidnaps, and displacing of approximately 7 million individuals from their homes,"[88] and the conflict in Rwanda caused a genocide with almost one million victims.[89] Information online showing a substantial connection between an individual and any of the groups involved in the conflicts mentioned above could easily produce them grave harms. This, added to the pervasiveness of misrepresentation and inaccurate information online, and internet mob justice, might trigger harms that jeopardize reincorporation into civilian life, hindering the peace process.

81  Berzins, *supra* note 77.
82  Pierre-Luc Deziel, "Let's Not Dwell on the Past: The Right to Be Forgotten as more than a Romantic Revolution" (Chapter 5).
83  Eloise Gratton & Jules Polonetsky, "Droit a L'Oubli: Canadian Perspective on the Global Right to Be Forgotten Debate" (2017) 15:2 Colo Tech LJ at 356.
84  Mayer-Schönberger, *supra* note 79 at 87.
85  Gratton & Polonetsky, *supra* note 83 at 339.
86  Andrea Slane, "Search Engines and the Right to Be Forgotten: Squaring the Remedy with Canadian Values on Personal Information Flow" (2018) 55 Osgoode Hall LJ at 363.
87  Jeffrey Rosen, "The Right to Be Forgotten" (2011–2012) 64 Stan L Rev at 355.
88  Claudia Josi, "Accountability in the Colombian Peace Agreement: Are the Proposed Sanctions Contrary to Colombia's International Obligations" (2017) 46 Sw L Rev at 401–402.
89  Suhrke & Howard, *supra* note 28.

## 3.2 Online harms add to these reputational harms

A robust amount of literature discusses various types of online harms.[90] For example, public disclosure of private information about individuals often derives in reputational harms,[91] and these are far worse in the digital era as "internet ensures that damaging personal information is not forgotten."[92] As Citron explains, "online disclosures can produce permanent emotional and reputational damage."[93]

The RTBF has been suggested as a response to a wide scope of potential online harms stemming from public disclosures of information.[94] Some have examined the RTBF as a tool to protect victims from information related to the wrongs they suffered being available permanently.[95] Others have focused on the RTBF as an instrument to protect the reputation of people who were convicted for criminal offenses to facilitate their reincorporation into society.[96] Similarly, case-law such as *Google Spain* has applied the RTBF to protect individuals' reputation derived from past negative financial information.[97]

In these cases, the RTBF was considered a suitable tool to protect individuals from reputational harms stemming from negative past information about them being publicly available online. However, reputational harms not only derive from embarrassing events, past debts, or criminal records. Indeed, under the General Data Protection Regulation (GDPR), the RTBF is of particular importance when search result links may put the subject of the information at risk.[98]

Online harms can certainly stem from extraordinary, traumatic circumstances, such as peace processes, for the actors involved in a past conflict. Former members of armed forces, as described above, are

90  See Ignacio N. Cofone, "Online Harms and the Right to Be Forgotten" (Chapter 1) for a survey.
91  Danielle Keats Citron, "Mainstreaming Privacy Torts" (2010) 98:6 Cal L Rev at 1812.
92  Ibid at 1813.
93  Ibid at 1814.
94  Gratton & Polonetsky, *supra* note 83 at 3.
95  Edward Lee, "The Right to Be Forgotten v. Free Speech" I/S: A Journal of Law and Policy for the Information Society (forthcoming) at 3.
96  Slane, *supra* note 86 at 387.
97  *Google Spain, SL, Google Inc v Agencia Española de Protección de Datos (AEPD), Mario Costeja González*, C-131/12, [2014] ECR I-317.
98  Article 29 Working Party, *Guidelines on the Implementation of the Court of Justice of the European Union Judgment on "Google Spain and Inc v. Agencia Española de Protección de Datos (AEPD) and Mario Costeja González" C-131/12*, 14/ENWP 225 (2014).

often subject to a multiplicity of online harms,[99] including reputation but also financial harm, discrimination, and in some contexts, as the Rwanda conflict illustrates, physical safety.

Having information online, out of context, available worldwide, and easily accessible connecting members of armed forces to the conflict could derive in discrimination or stigmatization of individuals. That could produce individual negative consequences such as unemployment and lack of physical safety that impede their reincorporation into civilian life and reconciliation and, perhaps more importantly, the anticipation of such consequences may lead groups not to accept a peace process leading to the perpetuation of conflicts that continue to tear societies apart. In the worst-case scenario, this could trigger another conflict. This problem is already visible in several conflicts, such as the ones we mention above, and will continue to intensify as future conflicts take place in a social context of widely available information that facilitates reputational harms. Absent an effective reincorporation and reconciliation process, neither a lasting peace can be achieved, nor can guarantees of non-recurrence be given.

This is detrimental to the likelihood of them agreeing to reintegration in the first place, and the sustainability of the peace thereafter. Just as the dissemination of negative financial information about an individual could affect his or her creditworthiness, or the availability of criminal records could hinder the employability of a former convict, information about an individual linking him or her with an armed conflict that a society is trying to overcome could affect their process of reincorporation into civilian society and reconciliation.

The RTBF is already applied to other social situations where reputational harms are at stake (embarrassing pictures, negative financial past, etc.). The application of such tool to peace processes may similarly reduce the risk of harms by reducing accessibility, dissemination, and availability of information about them posted online connecting them to the armed conflict. In these cases, the RTBF could be used to reduce harm toward these individuals in order to transition to a more sustainable peace.

Of course, the RTBF can neither ensure the eradication of such reputational harms nor, much less, can ensure reconciliation. But, depending on the legal and social context, it may be one piece in a much bigger puzzle that balances the different societal interests involved.

---

99  See Ignacio N. Cofone, "Online Harms and the Right to Be Forgotten" (Chapter 1) for a more detailed account of online harms.

## 3.3 Criminal law parallels

In what may be a closer analogy to the situation we analyze, the "right to forget" has historically been applied to convicted individuals to expunge their criminal records, sometimes including other information about the crime of which they were accused after they have served their sentence.[100] Indeed, as Stoddart mentions, some version of the RTBF started in France and Italy with granting some former prisoners a type of pardon that "included the removal of the notation of their criminal conviction from official records."[101] Other civil law jurisdictions, such as Germany, also allow courts to "suppress the name of convicted criminals from news accounts after paying their debt to society, as a right to privacy and policy of re-socialization."[102] The purpose of these rules was to help former convicts reintegrate into society absent reputational harms from their conviction.[103]

Some version of the RTBF has also been applied to individuals who are alleged to have committed a crime but where the criminal action prescribed or was extinguished.[104] Although convicted individuals and individuals whose alleged crime prescribed are different from individuals who were granted amnesty in many ways, there are some important similarities. The effects of their legal situations are comparable: for all three, criminal liability no longer exists (albeit for different reasons). In the case of convicts, this is because the sanction imposed was completed. In the cases of prescription and amnesty, this is because criminal liability is extinguished – in the former by time and the latter by amnesty.

Some common law jurisdictions currently have similar processes. In the United States,[105] a number of state courts grant expungement by

100 Rosen, *supra* note 87 at 88; W Gregory Voss & Celine Castel Renard, "Proposal for an International Taxonomy on the Various Forms of the 'Right to Be Forgotten': A Study on the Convergence of Norms", (2016) 14 Colo Tech LJ at 299–302.
101 See Jennifer Stoddart, "Lost in Translation: Transposing the Right to Be Forgotten from Different Legal Systems" (Chapter 2).
102 Michael J. Kelly & David Satola, "The Right to Be Forgotten" (2017) U Ill L Rev at 27.
103 See Martine Herzog-Evans, "Judicial Rehabilitation in France: Helping with the Desisting Process and Acknowledging Achieved Desistance" (2011) 3:1 Eur J Probation at 4–19; Steven Bennett, "The "Right to Be Forgotten": Reconciling EU and US Perspectives", (2012) 30 Berkeley J Intl L 161.
104 Tribunal Superior de Bogotá, Sala Penal [Superior Criminal Tribunal of Bogotá], Bogotá, 14 Jul 2016 (2016), *Martha Arango Barrera* (Colombia).
105 The history of these cases comes from *Melvin v. Reid*, 297 P. 112 Cal. App. 285, 91 (Cal CA 1931), where the court ordered creators of a movie to avoid using the

balancing the benefits of expungement with the public and government interest in retaining records.[106] In Ireland, the Spent Convictions and Certain Disclosures Act of 2016 allows for expunging records, with the exclusion of some crimes.[107] Similarly, going beyond expungement, the English High Court recently upheld an injunction to prevent the leakage of the new identity or re-identifiable personal information of two people convicted of murder after they were released from detention, under the argument that their physical safety may otherwise be at risk, in a judgment that draws attention to how social media would increase the risk of harm.[108]

The aim of an amnesty to former members of armed forces is their reincorporation into society as well. Both former convicts and amnestied individuals are in a process of reincorporating into society that is made more difficult by information about their amnesty or prison term being available.

The other side of the equation is also similar. While, in criminal justice, the rights of victims and rights of convicts and accused are best not seen as being in conflict,[109] victims may have an interest in such information. The difference in this regard between convicts and amnestied individuals is that the amnestied did not go through a criminal process that found them guilty. This difference operates both ways. On the one hand, victims of the conflict did not receive a truth-seeking

name of the acquitted individual whose trial the movie was based on, focusing on rehabilitation, and *Briscoe v. Reader's Digest Association, Inc.*, 483 P (2d) 34, 93 Cal Rptr 866, 4 Cal. (3d) 529 (1971), where the court held that the publication's reference to the plaintiff's prior crimes might infringe his ability to rehabilitate. The precedent was overturned on speech grounds in *Gates v. Discovery Communications, Inc.* 101 P (3d) 552, 34 Cal 4th 679, 21 Cal Rptr. (3d) 663 (2004). See Alessandro Mantelero, "The EU Proposal for a General Data Protection Regulation and the roots of the "right to be forgotten"" (2013) 29:3 Computer L & Sec Report 229.

106 See Brian Murray, "A New Era for Expungement Law Reform? Recent Developments at the State and Federal Levels" (2016) 10 Harv L & Pol'y Rev 361. At the federal level, this is applied in few cases such as some convictions of simple possession. See Anna Kessler, "Excavating Expungement Law: A Comprehensive Approach" (2015) 76 Temp L Rev at 425.

107 See TJ McIntyre & Ian O'Donnell, "Criminals, Data Protection, and the Right to a Second Chance" (2017) 58 Irish Jurist at 34. The excluded crimes include murder and most sexual offenses.

108 *Venables & Anor v News Group Papers Ltd & Ors,* [2019] EWHC 494 (Fam). See also *Venables v News Group Newspapers Ltd,* [2001] EWHC 430 QBD 32; *Venables v News Group Newspapers Ltd,* [2010] EWHC B18 (QB).

109 See Marie Manikis, "A New Model of the Criminal Justice Process: Victims' Rights as Advancing Penal Parsimony and Moderation" (2019) 30:201 Crim LF at 218–222.

criminal process to identify who is guilty for the crimes against them. On the other hand, not all amnestied will be guilty of all crimes, and some amnestied may be guilty of only minor crimes; we do not know who did what. Therefore, it may be inappropriate to put the full onus of victims' right on them when it harms both their individual rights and reconciliation.

## 4 Challenges and limitations to applying the RTBF in peace processes

### *4.1 Tension with free speech and access to information*

A large body of literature highlights the RTBF's tension with free speech and access to information.[110] Free speech can be defined as the ability to discuss matters of public concern.[111] Rosen, among many others, states that the RTBF currently "represents the biggest threat to free speech."[112] Scassa similarly argues that delisting information restricts the expressive rights of publishers of content as it makes information hard to find, and of searchers because it restricts their access to information.[113]

A key concern raised in this regard is that the RTBF can lead to over-deleting or over-delisting causing the disappearance of socially relevant information such as historical material.[114] In its delisting version, this may occur because of the RTBF eventually imposing burdensome responsibilities and financial liability to search engines and, to avoid liability, search engines might remove most information when requested, creating chilling effects.[115]

A society's receptivity to the RTBF, to some extent, depends on the value it places on free speech relative to privacy. Amy Lai evaluates

---

110 See e.g. Lee, *supra* note 95; Jasmine E McNealy, "The Emerging Conflict between Newsworthiness and the Right to Be Forgotten" (2012) 39:2 N Ky L Rev 119; Carbone, *supra* note 76; Fiona Brimblecombe & Gavin Phillipson, "Regaining Digital Privacy: The New Right to Be Forgotten and Online Expression" (2018) 4 Can J of Comp & Contemp L 1.
111 Robert Post, "The Constitutional Concept of Public Discourse: Outrageous Opinion, Democratic Deliberation, and Hustler Magazine v. Falwell" (1990) 103:3 Harv L Rev at 626.
112 Rosen, *supra* note 87 at 88.
113 See Teresa Scassa, "A Little Knowledge Is a Dangerous Thing?: Information Asymmetries and the Right to Be Forgotten" (Chapter 3).
114 Gratton & Polonetsky, *supra* note 83 at 343.
115 Ibid at 344–345.

that RTBF is better-received in Europe, where privacy is seen as more closely related to individuals' dignity than it is in other jurisdictions,[116] whereas the United States is reluctant to accept the RTBF by prioritizing speech.[117] This goes in line with James Whitman's idea of a transatlantic clash between American and continental European jurisdictions rooted on their different conceptions of privacy.[118]

Some jurisdictions undergoing peace processes have paved the way for the application of the RTBF, albeit in more usual contexts such as reputation. For example, in Colombia, it has been recognized and applied by courts in social security information, financial information, and criminal records.[119] That said, just because a country has been receptive to the application of the RTBF in tort law, criminal law, and financial regulation that does not mean it would in its peace process.

Speech and access to information may be more important during peace processes than during normal times. The Inter-American Commission on Human Rights, for example, has stated that free speech and access to information are important in transitional periods as they ensure victims' rights.[120] This concern, moreover, is frequently seen as having heightened importance for information related to war crimes and gross human rights violations.[121]

### 4.2 *Tension with truth, justice, and historical memory*

In peace processes, the RTBF might be in tension with other rights not present in the usual situations in which it is applied; namely, truth, justice, and historical memory. Although the application of the right in peace processes has not yet been discussed, general criticisms toward

---

116 Amy Lai, "The Right to Be Forgotten and What the Laws Should/Can/Will Be: Comparing the United States and Canada" (2017) 6 Global J Comp L at 85.

117 Ibid at 86; Robert Post, "Data Privacy and Dignitary Privacy: Google Spain, the Right to Be Forgotten, and the Construction of the Public Sphere" (2018) 67:5 Duke LJ 981.

118 James Q Whitman, "The Two Western Cultures of Privacy: Dignity versus Liberty" (2004) 113:6 Yale LJ at 1160–1161. See also Gregory Voss "Obstacles to Transatlantic Harmonization of Data Privacy Law in Context," (2019) Ill J L Tech & Pol'y.

119 See Valentina Manrique Gómez, "El Derecho al Olvido: Análisis Comparativo de las Fuentes Internacionales con la Regulación Colombiana" (2015) Revista de Derecho Comunicaciones y Nuevas Tecnologías at 8–9; Ingrid Carolina Forero Cardozo, "¿Existe el Derecho al Olvido en Internet en Colombia?, ¿Con Qué Derecho Entraría en Conflicto?" (2017) Universidad Católica de Colombia at 34.

120 Inter-American Commission on Human Rights, *supra* note 14 at 50–52.

121 Corte Constitucional [Constitutional Court], 2018, *Constitutionality of Law 1820, 2016 C-007/18* (Colombia) para 740.

amnesties themselves manifest concerns about preserving information that are also applicable to the RTBF.

Peace processes aim to help war-torn societies come to terms with a violent past,[122] placing the victims at the center of the processes.[123] The set of judicial and non-judicial mechanisms employed in these processes aim to fulfill victim reparation through truth-seeking, justice, and the preservation of history.[124]

The right to the truth's purpose is to "establish the facts and provide an overview of the past and violations by focusing on the historical, political, economic and social context in which abuses were perpetrated."[125] Teitel understands truth as "a virtue of justice."[126] Through truth-seeking processes, victims can be recognized as such,[127] publicly tell their stories, and confront offenders.[128] These processes help victims learn the whereabouts of disappeared family members, as well as what happened to them.[129] As such, they serve as the basis for reparation.[130] Truth commissions are an example of truth-seeking tools that investigate wrongdoings and make recommendations aimed at non-recurrence.[131]

The right to truth is connected to the right to history, which seeks to uncover the historical facts about abuses.[132] Since revealing the truth avoids that it gets deformed through time, doing so fosters the reconstruction of history.[133] Indeed, critics of the RTBF in private law contexts have argued that it interferes with history.[134] This problem is amplified in peace processes, where reducing information about the conflict may mean reducing information about a crucial part of that society's history.

The conception of victims' right to justice has changed through the history of transitional justice, evolving from a model directly related

122 United Nations, Security Council, The rule of law and transitional justice in conflict and post-conflict societies, Report of the Secretary -General (2004) at 4.
123 La Rosa & Xavier Philippe, *supra* note 17 at 370.
124 Ibid at 371.
125 La Rosa & Xavier Philippe, *supra* note 17 at 371.
126 Teitel, *supra* note 71 at 89.
127 La Rosa & Xavier Philippe, *supra* note 17 at 371.
128 Ho-Won Jeong, *Peacebuilding in Postconflict Societies, Strategy and Process* (Boulder, CO: Lynne Rienner Publishers, 2005) ch 6 *Reconciliation and Social Rehabilitation* at 163–164.
129 La Rosa & Xavier Philippe, *supra* note 17 at 376.
130 Jeong, *supra* note 128 at 164.
131 Report of the Secretary General, *supra* note 122 at 17.
132 La Rosa & Xavier Philippe, *supra* note 17 at 372.
133 Ibid at 371.
134 Gratton & Polonetski, *supra* note 83 at 343–346.

to offenders' accountability, to a restorative approach beyond punishments where the goal became healing societies in the pursuit of peace and reconciliation.[135] Under the second model, both the applications of amnesties and of truth-seeking mechanisms like truth commissions increased.[136] Justice in transitional justice contexts is not only achieved by legal processes such as sanctions and trials but also through informal mechanisms like apologies and commemorations.[137]

The two opposite approaches to transitional justice are "complete justice" and "clean slate."[138] While forgetting is often considered a mechanism to overcome a painful past, many question whether amnesties that produce insufficient accountability can produce an effective reconciliation.[139] Similarly, in criticizing amnesties themselves, others argue that forgetting is not a solid base on which to build a lasting peace and holding offenders accountable, providing reparations, and revealing the truth are key to ensure non-recurrence.[140] Some argue, moreover, that historical memory is key to avoiding impunity.[141] The RTBF may indeed have a negative impact on any form of historical memory.[142]

This point reflects an implicit concern regarding eventual violations of victims' rights. This does not, however, imply that harms will be produced in all circumstances or jurisdictions. It is crucial to acknowledge the risks that the application of the RTBF to past perpetrators involved in a conflict could represent to victims' rights in order to develop an approach that is respectful of them.

## 5 How the RTBF could be implemented in peace processes

### 5.1 For amnestied individuals

Based on the considerations set out so far, how can a post-conflict society construct the form and scope of the RTBF to reconcile: (i) free speech and access to information; (ii) victims' right to truth, justice,

135 Ruti G. Teitel, "Transitional Justice Genealogy" (2003) 16 Harv Hum Rts J at 77.
136 Ibid at 79, 82.
137 Roman David, "What We Know about Transitional Justice: Survey and Experimental Evidence" (2017) 38 Advances in Political Psychology at 153.
138 Zazueta, *supra* note 15 at 30–31.
139 Ibid at 31.
140 Zambrano, *supra* note 6 at 123.
141 Edet & Kooffreh, *supra* note 70 at 142.
142 Antoon De Baets, "A Historian's View of the Right to Be Forgotten" (2016) 30:1 Intl Rev L Comp & Tech at 61.

and history; and (iii) reincorporation into civilian society, so that reconciliation can be attained?

We suggest that the RTBF would not be applicable to all perpetrators. In particular, the RTBF should be considered only for amnestied individuals, and only within the scope of a lawful amnesty as a matter of international law, building on the existing balance among different interests that the society involved has struck for its peace process.

For example, the RTBF would likely be unfeasible with respect to information related to war crimes or gross human rights violations as denying or restricting access to this type of information would seriously affect victims' rights.[143] Similarly, it could be unfeasible for leaders of groups responsible for the wrongs in question. Information about these individuals connecting them to an armed conflict could be key to the truth about the conflict and victims' fate. However, this is not necessarily the case for amnesties recognized as legitimate by the international community. If a lawful amnesty were granted for political offenses, crimes connected to the conflict that do not constitute war crimes or gross human rights violations, or to low-rank members of rebel groups, then restricting accessibility or availability of personal information about those individuals may be compatible with victims' rights. Because the granting of amnesties is an exercise in balancing these values, granting the RTBF to individuals who did not receive amnesties would upset that balance; but considering its application as riders to those amnesties would rather build on it.

As we mentioned above, amnesties are considered a "form of legal oblivion,"[144] and the idea of forgetting is not alien to the processes in which they are applied.[145] If such amnesties are legitimate, and a group of actors involved in the conflict were considered eligible for favorable treatment in view of reconciliation, this consideration paves the path to consider amnestied individuals to be eligible for the RTBF. If amnesties are implemented as a tool to promote reintegration without interfering with victims' rights, then it is likely that the use of the RTBF to secure such reintegration will further that objective. Amnesties in peace processes are controversial in themselves and, in certain institutional

---

143 See Hugo A. Relva, "Three Propositions for a Future Convention on Crimes against Humanity: The Prohibition of Amnesties, Military Courts, and Reservations," (2018) 16:4 J Intl Criminal Justice, 857 at 860–868 for normative considerations on not granting amnesties for crimes against humanity.

144 Della Morte, *supra* note 67 at 431.

145 The sole granting of an amnesty indicates, to some extent, that the jurisdiction adopted a particular approach in peace processes toward a set of individuals.

contexts, a tailored application of the RTBF may be neither more nor less controversial than the amnesty it rests on.

## 5.2 Delisting

Any peace process seeks to balance the collective right to peace and victims' right to truth, justice, and history.[146] Therefore, any application of the RTBF in peace processes should also seek to harmonize victims' rights with the pursuit of reconciliation so that peace can be achieved sustainably. In striving for such balance, delisting may be the type of RTBF best-suited for a peace process. In particular, delisting references to amnestied individuals' past membership and information connecting them to the acts they received amnesty for from search engines. In other words, if someone searched for the name of an amnestied individual, no information related to his or her past as a member of the armed group or the crimes he or she received amnesty for would be listed on the search engine results. But such information would not be deleted from the source.

Erasing historical information would likely interfere with victims' rights. In Colombia, for instance, if information about all former FARC members connecting them to the conflict were deleted, this would likely violate victims' rights to justice by eliminating accountability. As there would be no clarification regarding the fate of victims' family members who were kidnapped or murdered during the conflict, it would violate victims' rights to the truth. And information necessary to rebuild the origins and circumstances that lead to the armed conflict would be destroyed, violating the right to historical memory.

Some highlight that guaranteeing access and preserving information during transitional justice avoid the destruction of history.[147] Information about the origins and circumstances that lead to the conflict or about disappeared individuals will likely always be adequate and relevant in peace processes. Nonetheless, the point above does not exclude the possibility of restricting access of the public to certain types of information about some members of armed forces.[148]

The rationale behind delisting is compatible with the situation of amnestied individuals. Since the information would not be deleted from the source, but rather its circulation would be reduced, delisting

146  Zazueta, *supra* note 15 at 21.
147  Constitutional Court, *supra* note 121 at para 740.
148  Ibid.

would be less likely to interfere with victims' reparation. It has been argued before that delisting does not threaten free speech and access to information as much as erasure may because the information remains at source.[149]

Moreover, delisting is the version of the RTBF sometimes applied to former convicts regarding their criminal records or information about the crime they were accused of in addition to expungement.[150] The purpose of restricting circulation of negative information about former convicts, or individuals who are alleged to have committed a crime for which the criminal action has prescribed, is to avoid that they bear the potentially significant negative consequences of society's reactions to the accusations.[151] This same reason is applicable to amnestied individuals. Unlike former convicts, individuals who are granted amnesty are not criminals, as any criminal offense they may or may not have committed is extinguished, preventing both proof of guilt and of innocence.[152] Moreover, the risks of reputational harms are greater to amnestied individuals than to the others given the connection they have with a violent armed conflict.[153]

An added advantage of applying this version of the RTBF in amnesties over other versions is that one of the main criticisms to it does not apply in this context. A common concern for delisting is the discretion that is given to private parties such as Google in deciding what is relevant and what serves the public purpose.[154] In applying the RTBF in peace processes, however, the discretional decision about what information should be delisted is already made. Some discretion would still exist at the edges in defining what information pertains to the conflict and which does not, but private entities would not be deciding what is irrelevant or what serves a public purpose.

---

149 Daphne Keller, "The Right Tools: Europe's Intermediary Liability Laws and the EU 2016 General Data Protection Regulation" 33.1 Berkeley Tech LJ 287 (2018) at 324–326; Article 29 Data Protection Working Party, *supra* note 98 at 5.
150 Rosen, *supra* note 87 at 88.
151 Ibid at 12–13.
152 See Louise Mallinder, *Amnesty, Human Rights and Political Transitions* (Oxford: Hart Publishing, 2008) at 111–113.
153 For an analysis of the right to privacy during armed conflicts under international law, see Asaf Lubin, "The Right to Privacy and Data Protection under IHL and HRL," in Robert Kolb, Gloria Gaggioli Gasteyger, and Pavle Kilibarda, eds, *Research Handbook on Human Rights and Humanitarian Law* [Edward Elgar, forthcoming 2020].
154 See e.g. Jemima Kiss, "Dear Google: Open Letter from 80 Academics on 'Right to Be Forgotten'", *The Guardian* (May 14, 2015).

## 5.3 Non-interference with public interest

Finally, this version of the RTBF should only be considered for certain kinds of information. A key aspect to applying the RTBF during peace processes is the scope of public interest and the extent to which information may be relevant. There are good reasons to believe that there is a substantive public interest in the remembrance of information pertaining to a society's internal conflict. Being the subject of considerable controversy can indeed be a factor to consider information of public interest.[155] Information pertaining to national conflicts that divide society is undoubtedly so.

As Slane points out, "the question is not whether the underlying information serves or has served the public interest in the abstract, but whether its continued *uncorrected* availability in search results related to an individual's name is in the public interest."[156] Therefore, one ought to ask what information about a conflict is undoubtedly relevant or of national interest. The relevance standard from *Google Spain* could be useful to some extent in determining which information should be delisted. In the case, the European Court of Justice (ECJ) provided that data subjects could request search engines to delist information if such information is "inadequate, irrelevant or no longer relevant, or excessive in relation to the purposes it was collected or processed."[157] Based on this standard, if the information at stake about amnestied individuals is relevant or necessary to reveal the truth, for example, about what happened to victims' family members who were kidnapped, then it should not be delisted.

In *Google Spain*, the ruling that the information was irrelevant rested on the idea that information at stake no longer represented who Mr. Costeja was then – it had turned misleading. In a peace process, what information will be misleading? Records have a historical value beyond the individuals involved in them; that is, beyond the assessment of whether a particular individual could come to produce similar harm again. For that reason, the RTBF should not conflict with State obligations to keep historical information. For example, it should not interfere with the amnestied individuals' obligations to provide information to truth commissions about, for example, historical facts about the conflict or information about missing persons.

155 Gratton & Polonetsky, *supra* note 83 at 383.
156 Andrea Slane, "Reconciling Privacy and Expression Rights by Regulating Profile Compilation Services" (Chapter 4).
157 Google Spain, *supra* note 97 at para 93. See also Scassa, *supra* note 133.

Based on this, some precision can be given about what information could or could not be delisted within amnesties. For example, information about war crimes and gross violations of human rights often occupies a special category in the international community.[158] The restriction of historical information about an individual responsible of war crimes or gross human rights violations would likely interfere with victims' rights.

Similarly, delisting information from governmental websites or websites from historical records would more likely interfere with the right to access information than it would to delink from other individuals' personal websites and blogs. This is because a central element of the right to access information is access to the information that is held by public entities. This said, the information that is undoubtedly relevant beyond historical records and should be kept publicly and easily accessible may be information about the collective, and not about the identification of each individual involved. It would be substantively different to grant a group the RTBF, erasing from search engines the groups' involvement with a series of crimes, than to grant it for individuals while keeping such references to the group.

However, within amnesties, public interest works both ways. Public interest has traditionally existed in the RTBF literature and jurisprudence as a limit or a counteracting factor to individuals' privacy, as something that may justify keeping the information regardless.[159] Similarly, for expungement, "[c]ourts most commonly utilize a balancing test to weigh the petitioner's rights against the public's interest in retaining the criminal records."[160] This element is radically different in the case under analysis. To the extent that the RTBF can aid reintegration and accelerate reconciliation, its application is done precisely in the interest of the public.

If the above conditions are fulfilled, depending on the social and institutional context, the RTBF could be applied in peace processes in a way that reconciles victims' rights, society's right to history, and offenders' reincorporation into society. The fulfillment of these conditions would contribute to a more effective reincorporation of groups into civilian life that avoids re-occurrence. "In the midst of the turmoil

---

158 Inter-American Commission on Human Rights, *supra* note 14 at 50–52; Constitutional Court, *supra* note 121 para 740.

159 Google Spain, *supra* note 97 at paras 98–99; Post, *supra* note 117 at 1039–1046, 1051–1054.

160 Anna Kessler, *supra* note 106 at 415. See also, e.g., *City of Pepper Pike v. Doe*, 66 Ohio St.(2d) 374, 421 N.E (2d) 1303 (1981).

of armed conflict, it might seem strange to discuss the right to privacy, let alone the right to data protection."[161] But it is precisely through the discussion of this right that the social values at stake can be better realized.[162]

## 6 Conclusion

The RTBF can aid peace processes in their pursuit of reconciliation. Peace processes face a credible commitment problem: armed forces' hesitation to believe they can effectively reincorporate into civilian life may lead them to reject peace agreements. That problem is worsened by technology, as the internet amplifies social harms that people who received amnesties will encounter. Information connecting amnestied individuals to an organization and a conflict that caused alarming amounts of harm available online to everyone could derive in discrimination or stigmatization producing unemployment and unsafety, among other consequences. If such harms jeopardize reincorporation into civilian life, they will render peace agreements within societies plagued by internal conflicts more difficult. Hindering reconciliation, in such way, hinders the peace process and any guarantees of non-recurrence.

If a society advances reconciliation as the most appropriate path to peace, the impact of these technologies must be acknowledged and post-conflict strategies must adapt to it. Although developed in different contexts, the RTBF may further the objectives that some peace processes aim to attain through amnesty programs for individuals who participated in the hostilities. The RTBF could be a useful mechanism to reduce the credible commitment problem by managing accessibility, dissemination, and availability of information connecting amnestied individuals with the armed conflict.

However, an emphasis on forgetting can run counter to other fundamental aspects of peace processes such as victim's rights and the preservation of historical truths. We thus propose a balanced approach in which post-conflict societies should consider the RTBF only under specific conditions. First, such approach would use delisting rather than deletion of compromising information found online, building on the RTBF applied to former convicts. Second, the RTBF should only be applicable to individuals who have received amnesties that

---

161  Lubin, *supra* note 153 at 1.
162  Ibid.

are recognized as legitimate by the international community regarding their connection to the events included in the amnesty. Third, the RTBF should not interfere with obligations to maintain information of heightened public interest about the conflict. Such a RTBF, in some institutional contexts, may facilitate reconciliation, guarantees of non-recurrence, and peace.

The RTBF as applied in peace processes is unprecedented. This approach does not guarantee a successful application, which will ultimately depend on how each social and institutional context balances truth and reconciliation. Determining this is a task for each jurisdiction. As with any mechanism of transitional justice, ultimately, it should be used only to the extent that it facilitates peace and the ending of human suffering.

# Bibliography

**Legislation**

*Act Respecting the Protection of Personal Information in the Private Sector,* CQLR c P-39.1, s 1.

*Business Practices and Consumer Protection Act,* SBC 2004, c 2.

*Canadian Charter of Rights and Freedoms,* s 7, Part I of the *Constitution Act, 1982,* being Schedule B to the *Canada Act 1982* (UK), 1982, c 11.

*Charter of Human Rights and Freedoms,* CQLR c C-12.

*Civil Code of Quebec,* CQLR c CCQ-1991.

Colombia, National Authority, Final Agreement to End the Armed Conflict and Build a Stable and Lasting Peace (2016).

*Colombian Amnesty Law 1820,* 2016.

Colombia's National Civil Registry, Results of the Plebiscite held on October 2, 2016 (October 2016), online: https://elecciones.registraduria.gov.co/pre_plebis_2016/99PL/DPLZZZZZZZZZZZZZZZZZZ_L1.htm

*Consumer Protection Act,* CQLR c P-40.1.

*Consumer Reporting Act,* RSO 1990, c C 33.

Decree 1391, 2016 (Colombia).

EC, *Corrigendum to Regulation (EU) 2016/679 of the European Parliament and of the Council of 27 April 2016 on the Protection of Natural Persons with Regard to the Processing of Personal Data and on the Free Movement of Such Data, and Repealing Directive 95/46/EC (General Data Protection Regulation),* [2018] OJ, L 127/1.

EC, *Regulation (EU) 2016/679 of the European Parliament and of the Council of 27 April 2016 on the Protection of Natural Persons with Regard to the Processing of Personal Data and on the Free Movement of Such Data, and Repealing Directive 95/46/EC (General Data Protection Regulation),* [2016] OJ, L 119/1.

EC, *Regulation 2016/679 of April 27, 2016 on the Protection of Natural Persons to the Processing of Personal Data and on the Free Movement of Such Data, and Repealing Directive 95/46/EC (General Data Protection Regulation),* [2016] OJ, L 119/1.

*Fair Credit Reporting Act,* 15 USC § 1681.

*Intimate Images and Cyber-protection Act*, NS Reg 101/2018, c 7.
*Intimate Images Protection Act*, RSNL 2018, c I-22.
Law 134, 1994 (Colombia).
*Personal Information Protection Act*, SA 2003, c P-6.5.
*Personal Information Protection Act*, SBC 2003, c 63.
*Personal Information Protection and Electronic Documents Act*, SC 2000, c 5.
*Protecting Victims of Non-consensual Distribution of Intimate Images Act*, RSA 2017, c P-26.9.
*Rehabilitation of Offenders Act 1974* (UK), c 53.
*The Intimate Image Protection Act*, CCSM c I87.


**Cases**

*Acosta Canada Corporation (Re)*, 2017 CanLII 29250 (AB OIPC).
*Alberta (Information and Privacy Commissioner) v United Food and Commercial Workers, Local 401*, 2013 SCC 62, [2013] 3 SCR 733.
*AT v Globe24h.com*, 2017 FC 114.
*Barrick Gold Corporation v Lopehandia et al.*, [2004] OJ No 2329, 239 DLR (4th) 577.
*Bodil Lindqvist v. Åklagarkammaren i Jönköping*, C-101/01, [2003] ECR I-12971.
*Briscoe v. Reader's Digest Association, Inc.*, 483 P (2d) 34, 93 Cal Rptr 866, 4 Cal. (3d) 529 (1971) Calo, Ryan *Digital Market Manipulation* (2014) 82 George Washington LR 996.
*Carpenter v. United States*, 585 US 138 S Ct 2206, 201 L Ed 2d 507.
*City of Pepper Pike v. Doe*, 66 Ohio St. (2d) 374, 421 N.E (2d) 1303 (1981).
*CL c BCF Avocats d'affaires*, 2016 QCCAI 114, 2016 CarswellQue 13743.
*Conrod v Caverley*, 2014 NSSC 35, 2014 CarswellNS 49.
Corte Constitucional [Constitutional Court], 2018, *Constitutionality of Law 1820, 2016 C-007/18* (Colombia).
*Douez v Facebook, Inc*, 2017 SCC 33, [2017] 1 SCR 751.
*Eastmond v Canadian Pacific Railway*, 2004 FC 852, 2004 CarswellNat 1842.
*Equustek Solutions Inc v Jack*, 2018 BCSC 610, 2018 CarswellBC 911.
*Fair Housing Council of San Fernando Valley v. Roommates.com LLC*, 521 F (3d) 1157 (9th Cir 2008).
*Ferenczy v MCI Medical Clinics*, 2004 CarswellOnt 1706, [2004] OJ No. 1775.
*Gates v. Discovery Communications, Inc.*, 101 P (3d) 552, 34 Cal 4th 679, 21 Cal Rptr. (3d) 663 (2004).
*Google Inc v Equustek Solutions Inc.*, 2017 SCC 34, [2017] 1 SCR 824.
*Google LLC v CNIL*, C–507/17, [2019] EUR-Lex CELEX No 62017CJ0507.
*Google LLC v Equustek Solutions Inc.*, Case No. 5:17-cv-04207-EJD (ND Cal 2017).
*Google Spain SL and Google Inc v Española de Protección de Datos (AEPD) and Mario Costeja Gonzalez*, CJEU C-131/12, [2014] ECR I-317, EUR-Lex CELEX No 62012CJ0131.
*Halton Catholic District School Board (Re)*, 2015 CanLII 13372 (ON IPC).

*In the Matter of a Reference Pursuant to Subsection 18.3(1) of the Federal Courts Act, RSC 1985, c F-7 of Questions and Issues of Law and Jurisdiction Concerning the Personal Information Protection and Electronic Documents Act, SC 2000, c 5 That Have Arisen in the Course of an Investigation into a Complaint Before the Privacy Commissioner of Canada*, 2019 FC 957 (CanLII).

*Isacov v Schwartzberg*, 2018 ONSC 5933, 2018 CarswellOnt 16828.

*Leduc v Roman*, 2009 CanLII 6838, [2009] OJ No 681.

*Matthew Herrick v Grindr Inc*, 765 Fed Appx 586 (2nd Cir 2019).

*Melvin v. Reid*, 297 P. 112 Cal. App. 285, 91 (Cal CA 1931).

*ML and WW v Germany*, No. 60798/10 and 65599/10 (28 June 2018).

*Nammo v TransUnion of Canada Inc*, 2010 FC 1284, 2010 CarswellNat 4908.

PIPEDA Report of Findings #2013–001, 2013 CanLII 3789 (PCC).

PIPEDA Report of Findings #2014–019, 2014 CanLII 99235 (PCC).

*Reference re subsection 18.3(1) of the Federal Courts Act, RSC 1985, c F-7,* 2019 FC 261(CanLII).

*R v Vu*, 2013 SCC 60, [2013] 3 SCR 657.

*Schuster v Royal & Sun Alliance Insurance Co of Canada*, 2009 CanLII 58971, [2009] OJ No 4518.

*Sparks v Dubé,* 2011 NBQB 040, 2011 CarswellNB 80.

*Spokeo Inc v Robins*, 136 S. Ct. 1540 (2016).

*Stacey Snyder v Millersville University et al.*, U.S. Dist. LEXIS 97943 (ED Pa 2008).

*State Farm Mutual Automobile Insurance Company v Privacy Commissioner of Canada*, 2010 FC 736, 2010 CarswellNat 2225.

*Stewart v Kempster*, 2012 ONSC 7236, 2012 CarswellOnt 16567.

Tribunal Superior de Bogotá, Sala Penal [Superior Criminal Tribunal of Bogotá], Bogotá, 14 July 2016 (2016), *Martha Arango Barrera* (Colombia).

US, *Federal Trade Commission, United States v Spokeo, Inc* (CV12–05001) (2012).

*Valiquette c Gazette*, 1996 CarswellQue 1156, [1997] RJQ 30.

*Venables & Anor v News Group Papers Ltd & Ors*, [2019] EWHC 494 (Fam).

*Venables v News Group Newspapers Ltd*, [2001] EWHC 430 QBD 32.

*Venables v News Group Newspapers Ltd*, [2010] EWHC B18 (QB).

**Books, Articles, and Reports**

Allen, Marshall, "Health Insurers Are Vacuuming Up Details About You — And It Could Raise Your Rates", *ProPublica* (17 July 2018).

Alvarez Berastegi, Amaia, "Transitional Justice in Settled Democracies: Northern Ireland and the Basque Country in Comparative Perspective" (2017) 10:3 Crit Stud on Terrorism 542.

Article 29 Working Party, *Guidelines on the Implementation of the Court of Justice of the European Union Judgment on "Google Spain and Inc v. Agencia Española de Protección de Datos (AEPD) and Mario Costeja González" C-131/12*, 14/ENWP 225 (2014).

Barocas, Solon & Selbst, Andrew D, "Big Data's Disparate Impact" (2016) 104 Cal L Rev 671.

Barrigar, Jennifer, "Submission: Office of the Privacy Commissioner of Canada Consultation – Online Reputation" (August 2016), online: *Office of the Privacy Commissioner of Canada*, https://www.priv.gc.ca/en/about-the-opc/what-we-do/consultations/consultation-on-online-reputation/submissions-received-for-the-consultation-on-online-reputation/or/sub_or_08/.

BC Freedom of Information and Privacy Association, "Submission to Consultation on Online Reputation (FIPA)" (August 2016), online: *Office of the Privacy Commissioner of Canada*, https://www.priv.gc.ca/en/about-the-opc/what-we-do/consultations/consultation-on-online-reputation/submissions-received-for-the-consultation-on-online-reputation/or/sub_or_13/.

Bennett, Steven C, "*The Right to Be Forgotten: Reconciling EU and US Perspectives*" (2012) 30:1 Berkeley J Int 161.

Bertram, Theo et al., "Three years of the Right to be Forgotten", online: https://elie.net/static/files/three-years-of-the-right-to-be-forgotten/three-years-of-the-right-to-be-forgotten-paper.pdf.

Berzins, Christopher, "Can the Right to be Forgotten Find Application in the Canadian Context?" (August 2016), online: https://www.priv.gc.ca/en/about-the-opc/what-we-do/consultations/consultation-on-online-reputation/submissions-received-for-the-consultation-on-online-reputation/or/sub_or_06/.

Berzins, Christopher, "Publicity and Privacy in Administrative Adjudication: A Right to be Forgotten" (2011) 39 Adv Q 1.

Binder, Nellie Veronika, "From the Message Board to the Front Door: Addressing the Offline Consequences of Race- and Gender-Based Doxxing and Swatting" (2018) 51 Suffolk UL Rev 55.

Blanchette, Jean-François, "The Noise in the Archive: Oblivion in the Age of Total Recall" in Serge Gutwirth, Yves Poullet, Paul De Hert & Ronald Leenes (eds), *Computers, Privacy and Data Protection: an Element of Choice* (New York: Springer, 2016).

Bloomberg Editorial Board, "The Unfinished Business of the Equifax Hack", *Bloomberg* (29 January 2019).

Bolton, Robert, "The Right to Be Forgotten: Forced Amnesia in a Technological Age" (2015) 31:2 J Marshall J Info Tech & Privacy L 133.

Bricker, Joe & Dhanji, Hana, Goswami, Manasvin & Marshall, Dave, "Response to the Notice of Consultation and Call for Essays — Online Reputation" (August 2016), online: *Office of the Privacy Commissioner of Canada*, https://www.priv.gc.ca/en/about-the-opc/what-we-do/consultations/consultation-on-online-reputation/submissions-received-for-the-consultation-on-online-reputation/or/sub_or_10/.

Brimblecombe, Fiona & Phillipson, Gavin, "Regaining Digital Privacy: The New Right to Be Forgotten and Online Expression" (2018) 4 Can J Comp & Contemp 1.

Brodey, Inger SB, "On Pre-Romanticism or Sensibility: Defining Ambivalences" in Michael Ferber (ed), *A Companion to European Romanticism* (Hoboken, NJ: Wiley-Blackwell, 2005).

Brookman, Justin & GS Hans, "Why Collection Matters: Surveillance as a De Facto Privacy Harm", *Centre for Democracy and Technology* (8 September 2013).

Brudholm, Thomas & Rosoux, Valerie, "The Unforgiving: Reflections on the Resistance to Forgiveness after Atrocity" in Alexander Keller Hirsch (ed), *Theorizing Post-Conflict Reconciliation* (Milton Park, Abingdon, Oxon: Routledge, 2012).

Bryson, Anna, "Victims, Violence, and Voice: Transitional Justice, Oral History, and Dealing with the Past" (2016) 39:2 Hastings Intl & Comp L Rev 299.

Calo, Ryan, "The Boundaries of Privacy Harm" (2011) 86:3 Ind LJ 2.

Campbell, Kirsten, "The Laws of Memory: The ICTY, the Archive, and Transitional Justice" (2013) 22:2 Soc & Leg Stud 247.

Carbone, Chelsea E, "To Be or Not to Be Forgotten: Balancing the Right to Know with the Right to Privacy in the Digital Age" (2015) 22 Va J Soc Pol & L 525.

Cavoukian, Ann, "Privacy by Design the 7 Foundational Principles" (January 2011), online: *Information and Privacy Commissioner of Ontario*, https://www.ipc.on.ca/wp-content/uploads/resources/7foundationalprinciples.pdf.

Citron, Danielle Keats, *Hate Crimes in Cyberspace* (Cambridge, MA: Harvard University Press, 2014).

Citron, Danielle Keats, "Mainstreaming Privacy Torts" (2010) 98:6 CLR 1805.

Citron, Danielle Keats, "Sexual Privacy" 128 Yale LJ 1870 (2019).

Cofone, Ignacio N, "Algorithmic Discrimination Is an Information Problem" (2019) 70:6 Hastings LJ 1389.

Cofone, Ignacio N, "Antidiscriminatory Privacy" (2019) 72 SMU L Rev 139.

Cofone, Ignacio N, "Google v. Spain: A Right to be Forgotten?" (2015) 15 Chicago-Kent J Intl & Comp L 1.

Cofone, Ignacio N, "Nothing to Hide, But Something to Lose" (2019) 70:1 UTLJ 64.

Cofone, Ignacio N & Robertson, Adriana, "Consumer Privacy in a Behavioral World" (2018) 69 Hastings LJ 1471.

Cofone, Ignacio N & Robertson, Adriana, "Privacy Harms" (2018) 69 Hastings LJ 1039.

Conitzer, Vincent, Taylor, Curtis R & Wagman, Liad, "Hide and Seek: Costly Consumer Privacy in a Market with Repeat Purchases" (2012) 31:2 Marketing Science 277.

Daigle, Thomas, "Europeans have a 'Right to Be Forgotten' Online. Should Canadians?" (26 September 2019), online: *Canadian Broadcasting Corporation News*, https://www.cbc.ca/news/technology/right-to-be-forgotten-canada-eu-court-1.5297528.

David, Roman, "What We Know About Transitional Justice: Survey and Experimental Evidence" (2017) 38 Advances in Political Psychology 151.

De Baets, Antoon, "A Historian's View of the Right to be Forgotten" (2016) 30:1 Intl Rev L Comp & Tech 57.

Della Morte, Gabriele, "International Law between the Duty of Memory and the Right to Oblivion" (2014) 14 Special Issue: Armenian Genocide Reparations Intl Crim L Re 427.

Delwaide, Karl & Guilmain, Antoine, "The "Right to be Forgotten" has a three-piece suit tailor-made in Canada? From Quebec to British Columbia" (2017) 14 CPLR 157.

Desforges, Alison, *Leave None to Tell the Story* (New York: Human Rights Watch, 1999).

Déziel, Pierre-Luc, *"Les limites du droit à la vie privée à l'ère de l'intelligence artificielle: groupes algorithmiques, contrôle individuel et cycle de traitement de l'information"* (2018) 30:3 CPI 829.

Edet, Joe & Kooffreh, B. E., "Transitional Justice in Post Conflict Societies: Underscoring the Debates on Amnesty versus Victims' Rights" (2018) 73 J L Pol'y & Globalization 139.

Els, Andrea Scripa, "Artificial Intelligence as a Digital Privacy Protector" (2017) 31:1 Harv JL & Tech 217.

Fair, Leslie, "Speaking of Spokeo: Part 1" *Federal Trade Commission* (12 June 2012), online: https://www.ftc.gov/news-events/blogs/business-blog/2012/06/speaking-spokeo-part-1.

Fearon, James D, "Commitment Problems and the Spread of Ethnic Conflict" in Lake, David & Rothchild, Donald (eds), *The International Spread of Ethnic Conflict* (Princeton, NJ: Princeton University Press, 1998).

Federal Trade Commission, "FTC, Nevada Obtain Order Permanently Shutting down Revenge Porn Site MyEx" (22 June 2018), online: *Federal Trade Commission*, https://www.ftc.gov/news-events/press-releases/2018/06/ftc-nevada-obtain-order-permanently-shutting-down-revenge-porn.

Fleischer, Peter, "Foggy Thinking About the Right to Oblivion", (9 March 2011), online: *Peter Fleischer: Privacy…?* http://peterfleischer.blogspot.com/2011/03/foggy-thinking-about-right-to-oblivion.html.

Forero Cardozo, Ingrid Carolina, *"¿Existe el Derecho al Olvido en Internet en Colombia?, ¿Con Qué Derecho Entraría en Conflicto?"* (2017) Universidad Católica de Colombia.

Franks, Mary Anne, "Sexual Harassment 2.0" (2012) 71 Md L Rev 655.

Fraser, David TS, "You'd Better Forget the Right to Be Forgotten in Canada" (August 2016), online: *Office of the Privacy Commissioner of Canada*, https://www.priv.gc.ca/en/about-the-opc/what-we-do/consultations/consultation-on-online-reputation/submissions-received-for-the-consultation-on-online-reputation/or/sub_or_07/.

Frishmann, Brett & Selinger, Evan, *Re-Engineering Humanity* (Cambridge: Cambridge University Press, 2018).

Gady, Franz-Stefan, "EU/U.S. Approaches to Data Privacy and the 'Brussels Effects': A Comparative Analysis" (2014) 15 Georgetown J of Intl Affairs 12

Gajda, Amy, "Privacy, Press, and the Right to be Forgotten in the United States" (2018) 93:201 Wash L Rev 201.

Geist, Michael, "Why a Canadian Right to Be Forgotten Creates More Problems Than It Solves" *The Globe and Mail* (26 January 2018).

Gomes, Ben, "Our Latest Quality Improvements for Search" (25 April 2017), online: *Google*, https://www.blog.google/products/search/our-latest-quality-improvements-search/.

Graves, Zachary, "The Dangerous Proliferation of the 'Right to Be Forgotten'", *Huffington Post* (18 August 2014).

Google Canada, "Can the Right to Be Forgotten Find Application in the Canadian Context and, If So, How?" (August 2016), online: *Office of the Privacy Commissioner of Canada*, https://www.priv.gc.ca/en/about-the-opc/what-we-do/consultations/consultation-on-online-reputation/submissions-received-for-the-consultation-on-online-reputation/or/sub_or_19/.

Google Transparency Report, "Search Removals under European Privacy Law" (30 May 2019), online: *Google*, https://transparencyreport.google.com/eu-privacy/overview?hl=en.

Gratton, Eloïse & Polonetsky, Jules, "Droit à l'oubli: Canadian Perspective on the Global 'Right to Be Forgotten' Debate" (2016) 15:2 Colo Tech LJ 337.

Gratton, Eloïse & Polonetsky, Jules, "Privacy above All Other Fundamental Rights? Challenges with the Implementation of a Right to Be Forgotten in Canada" (August 2016), online: *Office of the Privacy Commissioner of Canada*, https://www.priv.gc.ca/en/about-the-opc/what-we-do/consultations/consultation-on-online-reputation/submissions-received-for-the-consultation-on-online-reputation/or/sub_or_03/.

Gustafson, Karl E et al., "The Internet Never Forgets: Google Inc.'s "Right to Be Forgotten" EU Ruling and Its Implications in Canada" (August 2014), online: *McMillan LLP*, https://mcmillan.ca/mobile/The-Internet-Never-Forgets-Google-Incs-right-to-be-forgotten-EU-ruling-and-its-implications-in-Canada.

Harcourt, Bernard E, *Exposed. Desire and Disobedience in the Digital Age* (Cambridge, MA: Harvard University Press, 2015).

Hartzog, Woodrow, *Privacy's Blueprint: The Battle to Control the Design of New Technologies* (Cambridge, MA: Harvard University Press, 2018).

Hassan, Samer & de Filippi, Primavera, "The Expansion of Algorithmic Governance: From Code is Law to Law is Code" (2017) 17 The Journal of Field Actions 88.

Hazleton, William, "Look at Northern Ireland" in Timothy J. White (ed), *Lessons from the Northern Island Peace Processes* (Wisconsin: University of Wisconsin Press, 2013).

Hendel, John, "Why Journalists Shouldn't Fear Europe's "Right to be Forgotten"", *The Atlantic* (25 January 2012).

Herlocker, Jack, "Sidney Snyder and the Untruth that Won't Die", *Medium* (21 September 2015).

Herzog-Evans, Martine, "Judicial Rehabilitation in France: Helping with the Desisting Process and Acknowledging Achieved Desistance" (2011) 3:1 Eur J Probation 4.

IC, "Canada's Digital Charter: Trust in a Digital World" (25 June 2019), online: *Innovation Canada*, https://www.ic.gc.ca/eic/site/062.nsf/eng/h_00107.html).

IC, "Strengthening Privacy for the Digital Age" (21 May 2019), online: *Innovation, Science and Economic Development Canada*, https://www.ic.gc.ca/eic/site/062.nsf/eng/h_00107.html.

ICC, "Statement of ICC Prosecutor, Fatou Bensouda, on the Conclusion of the Peace Negotiations between the Government of Colombia and the Revolutionary Armed Forces of Colombia – People's Army" (1 September 2016), online: https://www.icc-cpi.int/Pages/item.aspx?name=160901-otp-stat-colombia.

Innovation, Science, and Economic Development Canada, Letter from the Minister to the Standing Committee on Access to Information, Privacy and Ethics (7 November 2019).

Innovation, Science and Economic Development Canada, "Strengthening Privacy in the Digital Age: Proposals to modernize the *Personal Information Protection and Electronic Documents Act*", Government of Canada (21 May 2019).

Jeong, Ho-Won, *Peacebuilding in Postconflict Societes, Strategy and Process* (United States of America: Lynne Rienner Publishers, 2005).

Josi, Claudia, "Accountability in the Colombian Peace Agreement: Are the Proposed Sanctions Contrary to Colombia's International Obligations" (2017) 46 Sw L Rev 401.

Kayitana, Evode, "Transitional Justice: Reconciling Domestic Amnesty with the Universal Jurisdiction of Foreign States" (2017) 8 Nnamdi Azikiwe U J Intl L & Juris 1.

Keating, Michael, "Northern Ireland and the Basque Country" in John McGarry (ed), *Northern Ireland and the Divided World: Post-Agreement Northern Ireland in Comparative* (Oxford: Oxford Scholarship Online, 2003).

Keller, Daphne, "A Right to be Forgotten in Canada?" (May 2018), online: *Center for Internet and Society*, http://cyberlaw.stanford.edu/blog/2018/05/right-be-forgotten-canada.

Keller, Daphne, "The Right Tools: Europe's Intermediary Liability Laws and the EU 2016 General Data Protection Regulation" 33.1 Berkeley Tech LJ 287 (2018).

Kelly, Michael J. & Satola, David, "The Right to be Forgotten" (2017) U Ill L Rev 1.

Kessler, Anna, "Excavating Expungement Law: A Comprehensive Approach" (2015) 76 Temp L Rev 403.

Kiss, Jemima, "Dear Google: Open Letter from 80 Academics on 'Right to Be Forgotten'", *The Guardian*, (May 14, 2015).

Koops, Bert-Jaap & Leenes, Ronald, "Privacy Regulation Cannot Be Hard-coded. A Critical Comment on the 'Privacy by Design' Provision in Data-Protection Law" (2011) 28:2 Intl Rev L Comp & Tech 159.

Kuperman, Alan J, *The Limits of Humanitarian Intervention: Genocide in Rwanda* (Washington, DC: Brookings Institution Press, 2004).

Lai, Amy, "The Right to Be Forgotten and What the Laws Should/Can/Will Be: Comparing the United States and Canada" (2017) 6 Global J Comp L 77.

Langlois, Ganaele & Slane, Andrea, "Debunking the Myth of "Not My Bad"": Sexual Images, Consent and Online Host Responsibilities in Canada" (2018) 30:1 CJWL 42.

Langlois, Ganaele & Slane, Andrea, "Economies of Reputation: The Case of Revenge Porn" (2017) 14:2 Comm & Crit/Cult Stud 120.

LaPlante, Lisa J, "Outlawing Amnesty: The Return of Criminal Justice in Transitional Justice Schemes" (2009) 49:4 Va J Intl L 915.

La Rosa, Anne-Marie & Philippe, Xavier, "Transitional Justice" in Vincent Chetail (ed), *Post-conflict Peacebuilding: A Lexicon* (Oxford: Oxford University Press, 2009).

Lee, Edward, "The Right to be Forgotten v. Free Speech", I/S: A Journal of Law and Policy for the Information Society (forthcoming).

Levin, Avner, "Privacy by Design by Regulation: The Case Study of Ontario" (2018) 4:1 Can J of Comp & Contemporary L 115.

Lewinsky, Monica, "The Price of Shame", *TED Talk* (20 March 2015).

Lomas, Natasha, "Google Super Successful at Spinning Europe's Right to be Forgotten as Farce", *TechCrunch* (4 July 2014).

Lubin, Asaf, "The Right to Privacy and Data Protection under IHL and HRL" in Robert Kolb, Gloria Gaggioli Gasteyger & Pavle Kilibarda (eds), *Research Handbook on Human Rights and Humanitarian Law* (Edward Elgar, forthcoming 2020).

Manikis, Marie, "A New Model of the Criminal Justice Process: Victims' Rights as Advancing Penal Parsimony and Moderation" (2019) 30:2 Crim LF 201.

Manrique Gómez, Valentina, *"El Derecho al Olvido: Análisis Comparativo de las Fuentes Internacionales con la Regulación Colombiana"* (2015) Revista de Derecho Comunicaciones y Nuevas Tecnologías.

Mantelero, Alessandro, "The EU Proposal for a General Data Protection Regulation and the Roots of the "Right to Be Forgotten"" (2013) 29:3 Computer L & Sec Report 229.

Marwick, Alice E, *Status Update: Celebrity, Publicity and Branding in the Social Media Age* (New Haven, CT: Yale University Press, 2013). ISBN: 978-0-300-19915-4.

Maxwell, Winston, "Top Human Rights Court Denies Right to be Forgotten in Old Murder Case", *Chronicle of Data Protection* (21 August 2018).

Mayer-Schöenberger, Viktor, *The Virtue of Forgetting in the Digital Age* (Princeton, NJ: Princeton University Press, 2009).

McGreal, Chris, "Rwanda Genocide 20 Years On: 'We Live with Those Who Killed Our Families. We Are Told They're Sorry, but Are They?" *The Guardian* (12 May 2013).

McIntyre, TJ & O'Donnell, Ian, "Criminals, Data Protection, and the Right to a Second Chance" (2017) 58 Irish Jurist 1.

McNealy, Jasmine E, "The Emerging Conflict between Newsworthiness and the Right to Be Forgotten" (2012) 39:2 N Ky L Rev 119.

Merle, Roger et Vitu, André. *Traité de droit criminel: procédure pénale*, 8th ed (Paris: Édition Cujas, 2000).

Microsoft, "Content Removal Requests Report", *Microsoft*, online: https://www.microsoft.com/en-us/corporate-responsibility/crrr.

Minow, Martha, *Between Vengeance and Forgiveness* (United States of America: Beacon Press, 1998).

Montreal Gazette Editorial, "Editorial: Is There a 'Right to Be Forgotten'?" *Montreal Gazette* (30 May 2014).

Mugshots, "Mugshots.com News" (30 May 2019), online: *Mugshots*, https://mugshots.com/.

Murray, Brian, "A New Era for Expungement Law Reform? Recent Developments at the State and Federal Levels" (2016) 10 Harv L & Pol'y Rev 361.

Ndong, P. K. A., "Infléchissement du droit à l'oubli et cohérence de la procédure pénale de traitement du délit de blanchiment de capitaux" (2017) BDE 2.

Nissenbaum, Helen, *Privacy in Context: Technology, Policy, and the Integrity of Social Life* (Stanford, CA: Stanford University Press, 2010).

Nuno Gomes de Andrade, Norberto, "Oblivion: The Right to be Different... from Oneself: Re-Proposing the Right to Be Forgotten" in Alessia Ghezzi, Angela Guimaräes Pereira & Lucia Vesnić-Alujević (eds), *The Ethics of Memory in a Digital Age: Interrogating the Right to Be Forgotten* (London: Palgrave Macmillan, 2014). ISBN 978-1-137–42845-5.

Ohmura, Hirotaka, "Termination and Recurrence of Civil War: Which Outcomes Lead to Durable Peace after Civil War?" (2011) 12:3 Japanese J P Sci 375.

OIPC BC, "Conducting Social Media Background Checks" (May 2017), online: *Office of the Information & Privacy Commissioner for British Columbia*, https://www.oipc.bc.ca/guidance-documents/1454.

Offstein, Norman, "An Historical Review and Analysis of Colombian Guerrilla Movements: FARC, ELN and EPL" (2003) 52 Desarrollo y Sociedad 99.

OPC, "Announcement: Privacy Commissioner Seeks Federal Court Determination on Key Issue for Canadians' Online Reputation" (10 October 2018), online: *Office of the Privacy Commissioner of Canada*, https://www.priv.gc.ca/en/opc-news/news-and announcements/2018/an_181010/.

OPC, *Data Brokers a Look at the Canadian and American Landscape: Report Prepared by the Research Group of the Office of the Privacy Commissioner of Canada* (Quebec: Office of the Privacy Commissioner of Canada, 2014).

OPC, "Draft OPC Position on Online Reputation" (26 January 2018), online: *Office of the Privacy Commissioner of Canada*, https://www.priv.gc.ca/en/about-the-opc/what-we-do/consultations/consultation-on-online-reputation/pos_or_201801/.

OPC, "Joint investigation of Facebook, Inc. by the Privacy Commissioner of Canada and the Information and Privacy Commissioner for British Columbia" (25 April 2019), online: *Office of the Privacy Commissioner of Canada*, https://www.priv.gc.ca/en/opc-actions-and-decisions/investigations/investigations-into-businesses/2019/pipeda-2019-002/.

OPC, "Notice of Consultation on Online Reputation" (21 January 2016), online: *Office of the Privacy Commissioner of Canada*, https://www.priv.gc.ca/en/about-the-opc/what-we-do/consultations/consultation-on-online-reputation/or_consultation/.

OPC, "Privacy and Social Networking in the Workplace" (December 2015), online: *Office of the Privacy Commissioner of Canada*, https://www.priv.gc.ca/en/privacy-topics/privacy-at-work/02_05_d_41_sn/.

OPC, "Privacy Commissioner Seeks Federal Court Determination on Key Issue for Canadians' Online Reputation" (10 October 2018), online: *Office of the Privacy Commissioner of Canada*, https://www.priv.gc.ca/en/opc-news/news-and-announcements/2018/an_181010/.

OPC, "Summary of Reputation Submissions" (20 December 2017), online: *Office of the Privacy Commissioner of Canada*, https://www.priv.gc.ca/en/about-the-opc/what-we-do/consultations/consultation-on-online-reputation/submissions-received-for-the-consultation-on-online-reputation/or/or_intro/.

OPC, "The Strategic Privacy Priorities" (2015), online: *Office of the Privacy Commissioner of Canada*, https://www.priv.gc.ca/en/about-the-opc/opc-strategic-privacy-priorities/the-strategic-privacy-priorities/#sa.

OPC, "2016 Survey of Canadians on Privacy" (January 2017), online: https://www.priv.gc.ca/en/opc-actions-and-decisions/research/explore-privacy-research/2016/por_2016_12/.

Organization of American States, Inter-American Commission on Human Rights, *Derecho a la Verdad en América* (2014).

Padova, Yann, "Le Droit à l'oubli, un droit universel?" (2016) 130 *Revue Lamy droit de l'immatériel* 34.

Pan, Sheri B, "Get to Know Me" (2016) 30:1 Harv JL & Tech 249.

Pasquale, Frank, "Reforming the Law of Reputation" (2015) 47:2 Loy U Chicago LJ 515.

Peguera, Miquel, "No More Right-To-Be-Forgotten For Mr. Costeja, Says Spanish Data Protection Authority" (3 October 2015), online: *The Center for Internet and Society*, http://cyberlaw.stanford.edu/blog/2015/10/no-more-right-be-forgotten-mr-costeja-says-spanish-data-protection-authority.

Post, Robert, "Data Privacy and Dignitary Privacy: Google Spain, the Right to Be Forgotten, and the Construction of the Public Sphere" (2018) 67:5 Duke LJ 981.

Post, Robert, "The Constitutional Concept of Public Discourse: Outrageous Opinion, Democratic Deliberation, and Hustler Magazine v. Falwell" (1990) 103:3 Harv LR 601Powles, Julia, "The Case That Won't Be Forgotten" (2015) 47 Loy U Chicago LJ 583.

Price, Nicholson W. & Cohen, I. Glenn, "Privacy in the Age of Medical Big Data" (2019) 25 Nature Medicine 37.

Privacy by Design Centre of Excellence, "The Seven Foundational Principles", *Ryerson University*, online: https://www.ryerson.ca/pbdce/certification/seven-foundational-principles-of-privacy-by-design/.

Provost, Rene, "FARC Justice: Rebel Rule of Law" (2018) 8 UC Irvine L Rev 227.

Reding, Viviane, "The Future of Data Protection and Transatlantic Cooperation" (Speech delivered at 2nd Annual European Data Protection and Privacy Conference, 6 December 2011).

Reding, Viviane, "The Upcoming Data Protection Reform for the European Union" (2011) 1 Intl Data Privacy L 3.

Reputation VIP, "Forget.me: découvrez la réalité du droit à l'oubli" (31 May 2019), online: *Reputation VIP*, https://www.reputationvip.com/fr/blog/forget-me-fr.

Roberts, Jessica L, "Protecting Privacy to Prevent Discrimination" (2014) 56 Wm & Mary L Rev 2097.

Rosen, Jeffrey, "The Right to Be Forgotten" (2011–2012) 64 Stan L Rev 88.

Rosenstock, Michael, "Is There a 'Right to Be Forgotten' in Canada's Personal Information Protection and Electronic Documents Act (PIPEDA)?" (2018) 14 CJLT 131.

Rouvroy, Antoinette, "Réinventer l'art d'oublier et de se faire oublier dans la société de l'information" in Stéphanie Lacour (ed), *La sécurité de l'individu numérisé. Réflexions prospectives et internationals* (Paris, L'Harmattan, 2008).

Rouvroy, Antoinette & Berns, Thomas, "Gouvernementalité algorithmique et perspectives d'émancipation. Le disparate comme condition d'émancipation par la relation?" (2013) 177:1 Réseaux 163.

Rouveroy, Antoinette & Berns, Thomas, "Le nouveau pouvoir statistique. Ou quand le contrôle s'exerce sur un réel normé, docile et sans événement car constitué de corps 'numériques'..." (2010) 40 Multitudes 88.

Rubinstein, Ira S, "Regulating Privacy by Design" (2011) 26:3 BTLJ 1409.

Rustad, Michael L. & Kulevska, Sanna, "Reconceptualizing the Right to Be Forgotten to Enable Transatlantic Data Flow" (2015) 28:2 Harv JL & Tech 349.

Sarkin, Jeremy & Daly, Erin "Too Many Questions, Too Few Answers: Reconciliation in Transitional Societies" (2004) Colum HRLR 661.

Scassa, Teresa, "Journalistic Purposes and Private Sector Data Protection Legislation: Blogs, Tweets, and Information Maps" (2010) 35 Queen's LJ 733.

Scassa, Teresa, "Right to Be Forgotten Reference to Federal Court Attracts Media Concern" (17 April 2019), online: *Teresa Scassa*, http://www.teresascassa.ca/index.php?option=com_k2&view=itemlist&task=user&id=63%3Ateresascassa&limitstart=10.

Silva, Miguel, "El camino hacia la prosperidad, el milagro colombiano", Report, (2015) Atlantic Council. Adrienne Arsht Latin American Center.

Skinner-Thompson, Scott, "Privacy's Double Standards" (2018) 93:4 Wash L Rev 2051.

Slane, Andrea, "Information Brokers, Fairness, and Privacy in Publicly Accessible Information" (2018) 4:1 Can J Contemporary & Comparative L 249.

Slane, Andrea, "Regulating Business Models that Capitalize on User Posted Personal Information of Others: How Can Canada's Privacy Regime Protect Victims of Online Shaming Businesses?" (August 2016), online: *Office of the Privacy Commissioner of Canada*, https://www.priv.gc.ca/en/about-the-opc/what-we-do/consultations/consultation-on-online-reputation/submissions-received-for-the-consultation-on-online-reputation/or/sub_or_01/.

Slane, Andrea, "Search Engines and the Right to Be Forgotten: Squaring the Remedy with Canadian Values on Personal Information Flow" (2018) 55:2 Osgoode Hall LJ 349.

Smith, Michee, "Updating our 'Right to Be Forgotten' Transparency Report" (26 February 2018), online: *Google*, https://blog.google/around-the-globe/google-europe/updating-our-right-be-forgotten-transparency-report/.

Solove, Daniel J, "Conceptualizing Privacy" (2002) 90 Cal L Rev 1087.

Sottas, Eric, "Transitional Justice and Sanctions" (2008) 90 Intl Rev Red Cross 371.

Spokeo, "What Results Will I See When I Do a Search?" (30 May 2019), on-line: *Spokeo*, https://www.spokeo.com/enterprise.

Standing Committee on Access to Information, Privacy and Ethics, "Towards Privacy by Design: Review of the Personal Information Protection and Electronic Documents Act" (February 2018), online: *House of Commons*, https://www.ourcommons.ca/DocumentViewer/en/42-1/ETHI/report-12/.

Stark, Luke, "Algorithmic Psychometrics and the Scalable Subject" (2008) 48:2 Social Studies of Science 204.

Suhrke, Astri & Adelman, Howard, *The Path of a Genocide: The Rwanda Crisis from Uganda to Zaire* (New York: Routledge, 1999).

Susser, Daniel, Roessler, Beate & Nissenbaum, Helen, "Technology, Autonomy, and Manipulation" (2019) 8:2 Internet Policy Rev 1.

Szoke-Burke, Sam, "Searching for the Right to Truth: The Impact of International Human Rights Law on National Transitional Justice Policies" (2015) 33:2 BJIL526.

Tashea, Jason, "Alleged Owners of Mugshots.com Charged in Extortion Scheme, Face Extradition to California", *ABA Journal* (18 May 2018).

Teitel, Ruti G, "Transitional Justice Genealogy" (2003) 16 Harv Hum Rts J 69.

Teitel, Ruti, *Transitional Justice* (New York: Oxford University Press, 2000).

The Globe and Mail, "Submission to the OPC's Consultation on Online Reputation" (August 2016), online: *Office of the Privacy Commissioner of Canada*, https://www.priv.gc.ca/en/about-the-opc/what-we-do/consultations/consultation-on-online-reputation/submissions-received-for-the-consultation-on-online-reputation/or/sub_or_22/.

Thomas Flores, Edward & Nooruddin, Irfan, "Credible Commitment in Post Conflict Recovery" in Coyne, Christopher J. &. Mathers, Rachel L. (eds), *The Handbook on the Political Economy of War* (Northampton, MA: Edward Edgar Publishing, 2011).

Tonge, Jonathan, *Comparative Peace Processes* (Cambridge: Polity Press, 2014).

Trudel, Pierre, "Effacer le passé: un droit?" *Le Devoir* (7 July 2018).

UN, Guidance Note of the Secretary-General, *United Nations Approach to Transitional Justice* (2010).

United Nations, Security Council, The Rule of Law and Transitional Justice in Conflict and Post-conflict Societies, Report of the Secretary-General (2004).

Vaidhyanathan, Siva, *Antisocial Media: How Facebook Disconnects Us and Undermines Democracy* (Oxford: Oxford University Press, 2018).

Vermeys, Nicolas, "Privacy v. Transparency: How Remote Access to Court Records Forces Us to Re-examine Our Fundamental Values" in Karim Benyekhlef et al. (eds), *eAccess to Justice* (Ottawa: University of Ottawa Press, 2016).

Villarraga Sarmiento, Alvaro, "Los acuerdos de paz Estado-Guerrillas en Colombia, 1982–2016" (2016) 14:28 Derecho y Realidad 109.

Voss, Gregory, "Obstacles to Transatlantic Harmonization of Data Privacy Law in Context", (2019) Ill J L Tech & Pol'y.

Voss, Gregory & Castel Renard, Celine, "Proposal for an International Taxonomy on the Various Forms of the 'Right to Be Forgotten': A Study on the Convergence of Norms" (2016) 14 Colo Tech L J 281.

Waldman, Ari, "Cybermobs Multiply Online Threats and Their Danger", *New York Times* (3 August 2016).

Waldman, Ari, "Queer Dating Apps Are Unsafe by Design: Privacy Is Particularly Important for L.G.B.T.Q. People", *New York Times* (20 June 2019).

Waldman, Ari, *Privacy as Trust. Information Privacy for an Information Age* (New York: Cambridge University Press, 2018).

Walter, Barbara F, "The Critical Barrier to Civil War Settlement" (1997) 51:3 Intl Org 335.

Warren, Samuel D & Brandeis, Louis D, "The Right to Privacy" (1890) 4:5 Harv L Rev 193.

Weber, Rolf, "The Right to Be Forgotten More Than a Pandora's Box?" (2011) 2 J of Intellectual Property, Information Technology and Electronic Commerce L 120.

Werro, Franz, "The Right to Inform v. the Right to be Forgotten: A Transatlantic Clash" in Aurelia C. Ciacchi et al., (eds), *Liability in the Third Millennium* (Baden-Baden, FRG: Nomos 2009) 285.

White, Timothy J, et al., "Extending Peace to the Grassroots: The Need for Reconciliation in Northern Ireland after the Agreement" in Timothy J. White (ed), *Lessons from the Northern Island Peace Processes* (Wisconsin: University of Wisconsin Press, 2013).

Whitman, James Q, "The Two Western Cultures of Privacy: Dignity versus Liberty" (2004) 113:6 Yale LJ 1151.

Whittaker, Zack, "Equifax Breach Was 'Entirely Preventable' Had It Used Basic Security Measures, Says House Report", *TechCrunch* (10 December 2018).

Zambrano Ramón, Gloria, "Memoria y Reparación: el Camino de la Justicia Transicional para las Víctimas" in Jairo Becerra (ed), *Fundamentación y aplicabilidad de la justicia transicional en Colombia* (Bogotá: Universidad Católica de Colombia, 2016).

Zarsky, Tal Z, "Privacy and Manipulation in the Digital Age" (2019) 30:1 Theoretical Inquiries in Law 15.

Zazueta Carrillo, Laura Wendy "The Right to the Truth in the Context of Transitional Justice as an Obligation of the Mexican State in the Face of Impunity" (2014) 9:2 VIeI 11.

Zillner, Sonja et al., "Big Data-Driven Innovation in Industrial Sectors" in José María Cavanillas, Edward Curry & Wolfgang Wahlster (eds), *New Horizons for a Data-Driven Economy. A Roadmap for Usage and Exploitation of Big Data in Europe* (New York City: Springer, 2016).

Zuboff, Shoshana, *The Age of Surveillance Capitalism: The Fight for a Human Future at the New Frontier of Power* (New York: Public Affairs Books, 2019).

Zuiderveen Borgesius, Frederik, et al., "Online Political Microtargeting: Promises and Threats for Democracy" (2018) 14:1 Utrecht L Rev 82.

# Index

Note: Page numbers followed by "n" denote endnotes.

For Product Safety Concerns and Information please contact our EU
representative  GPSR@taylorandfrancis.com
Taylor & Francis Verlag GmbH, Kaufingerstraße 24, 80331 München, Germany